RESEARCH METHODS
THE BASICS

Research Methods: The Basics is an accessible, user-friendly introduction to the different aspects of research theory, methods and practice. This second edition provides an expanded resource suitable for students and practitioners in a wide range of disciplines including the natural sciences, social sciences and humanities. Structured in two parts – the first covering the nature of knowledge and the reasons for research, the second the specific methods used to carry out effective research and how to propose, plan, carry out and write up a research project – this book covers:

- Reasons for doing a research project
- Structuring and planning a research project
- The ethical issues involved in research
- Different types of data and how they are measured
- Collecting and analysing qualitative and quantitative data in order to draw sound conclusions
- Mixed methods and interdisciplinary research
- Devising a research proposal and writing up the research
- Motivation and quality of work.

Complete with a glossary of key terms and guides to further reading, this book is an essential text for anyone coming to research for the first time.

Nicholas Walliman is Senior Lecturer in the School of Architecture at Oxford Brookes University, UK.

THE BASICS

RESEARCH METHODS

THE BASICS

Second edition

Nicholas Walliman

Routledge
Taylor & Francis Group

LONDON AND NEW YORK

Second edition published 2018
by Routledge
2 Park Square, Milton Park, Abingdon, Oxon OX14 4RN

and by Routledge
711 Third Avenue, New York, NY 10017

Routledge is an imprint of the Taylor & Francis Group, an informa business

First edition published by Routledge 2011

British Library Cataloguing-in-Publication Data
A catalogue record for this book is available from the British Library

Library of Congress Cataloguing-in-Publication Data
Names: Walliman, Nicholas, author.
Title: Research methods: the basics/by Nicholas Walliman.
Description: 2nd edition. | Abingdon, Oxon; New York, NY: Routledge, 2018.
Identifiers: LCCN 2017012356 | ISBN 9781138693982 (hardback) |
ISBN 9781138693999 (pbk.) | ISBN 9781315529011 (ebook)
Subjects: LCSH: Social sciences–Research–Methodology. | Humanities–
Research–Methodology.
Classification: LCC H62.W254 2018 | DDC 001.4/2–dc23LC record available at
https://lccn.loc.gov/2017012356

ISBN 978-1-138-69398-2 (hbk)
ISBN 978-1-138-69399-9 (pbk)
ISBN: 978-1-315-52901-1 (ebk)

Typeset in Bembo
by Sunrise Setting Ltd, Brixham, UK

MIX
Paper from
responsible sources
FSC   FSC™ C013985
www.fsc.org

Printed in the United Kingdom
by Henry Ling Limited

To Ursula

CONTENTS

FIGURES

TABLES

ACKNOWLEDGEMENTS

My grateful thanks go to Alma Clavin for allowing me to use an extract from her PhD thesis demonstrating a literature review, and Marina Muenchenbach for allowing me to use her master's research proposal to demonstrate aspects of research writing. Also thanks to Kirkegaard Associates for permission to use their photographs of the Festival Hall acoustic model and Jane Stiles for permission to use her photographs of the hospital waiting areas. I would also like to thank Adi Walker for allowing me to publish his interview template and Christopher Kendrick, Mina Samangooei, Victor Webster and Mariana Correia for the abstracts from their papers or dissertations, as well as Daniel Kozak for the excerpt from his thesis focussing on the meaning of concepts. I am also indebted to Alyson Claffey from Routledge for her patience and encouragement, and Denise Bannerman and Sharon Nickels for their work on production. My master's and doctoral students have also been an inspiration to me and gave me many insights into the practical problems of engaging in research and demonstrated ways to overcome them.

My greatest appreciation goes to my wife, Ursula, for her support and tolerance during the writing of this book.

INTRODUCTION

Doing a research project is a journey of discovery, not only as a way to reveal new knowledge and understanding about a particular subject, but also as a personal expedition into unknown territory that demands curiosity, imagination, creativity, enterprise and determination. That is why the writing of a dissertation or thesis is regarded as an effective exercise in both educational and personal development, and features as a stepping stone in the completion of courses in almost every subject. Of course, research is undertaken in other contexts too – professional, voluntary and out of sheer personal interest. The frustrations and rewards are there whichever reason you do it for. I have written this book to provide you with a basic guide to the research process that will make it easier for you to plan your project and help you to make important decisions on the way.

Research methods are the tools and techniques for doing research. Research is a term used liberally for any kind of investigation that is intended to uncover interesting or new facts. As with all activities, the rigour with which this activity is carried out will be reflected in the quality of the results. In this book, you will find a basic review of the nature of research and the methods that are used to undertake a variety of investigations relevant to a wide range of subjects such as the natural sciences, social science, social anthropology, psychology, politics, leisure studies and sport, hospitality, healthcare and nursing studies, the environment, business, education and the humanities.

Just about every university course includes an element of research that students must carry out independently, in the form of projects, dissertations and theses, and the more advanced the degree, the greater the research content. In the workplace, there is frequently a need to do research in order to develop or improve the business or service, while some types of businesses rely on doing research projects for their very existence.

Research methods are a range of tools that are used for different types of enquiry, just as a variety of tools are used for doing different practical jobs – for example, a pick for breaking up the ground or a rake for clearing leaves. In all cases, it is necessary to know what the correct tools are for doing the job, and how to use them to best effect. This book provides you with the basic information about the tools used in research and the situations in which they are applied; it also indicates briefly how they are used by giving practical examples.

I have also included chapters that describe the theoretical background to research and the ways of thinking that lead to the different ways of carrying out investigations and coming to conclusions. Therefore, the book is divided into two basic parts. Part I consists of Chapters 1–5 and provides an introduction to research theory and general practice. Part II contains Chapters 6–13; it explains the main research methods used for collecting and analysing data, and gives advice on the practical issues of presenting your research in a clear and attractive manner.

As this book acts as an introduction to the basics of research methods, you will probably want to find out more about many of the issues mentioned, so I have made suggestions for further reading at the end of each chapter ('Where to find out more'). I have added short comments on the content and style of the publications to provide some guidance. Generally, the most approachable books are mentioned first. You will notice that research is riddled with technical terms, or what some people would call jargon. The first time any of the terms are used they are highlighted in **bold** and then I normally provide an explanation of the meaning. In order to provide a useful way to remind you of the definitions of the main technical terms used in this book (and for that matter elsewhere too), I have included a glossary at the end which includes all those terms highlighted in bold in the main text plus a few extra ones you may come across in your other reading. You can easily refer to the glossary from anywhere in the book.

Not only will reading this book give you an insight into the different aspects of research theory and practice and help you to understand what is involved in carrying out a research project, it will also help you to evaluate the claims made by academics, experts of all kinds, politicians, advertisers, etc. by judging the quality of the evidence provided by the research on which they base their arguments.

You don't have to read the book from the beginning to the end, like a novel. It can be used as a reference for finding out about the characteristics of a specific research method, the meaning of a certain term or about aspects of theory. However, the chapters are arranged in the approximate sequence of the activities required for carrying out a research project, so it can be used as a step-by-step guide to doing your own research.

Finding out about things and trying to understand events and situations are activities that symbolize the very essence of humanity. At a time when we are bombarded with information, when pressing problems are ever present, when the opportunities for discovery are all around us, it is really useful, if not essential, to be familiar with the methods for doing research – any research. This book will help you to think clearly, to structure your enquiries and to come to conclusions based on appropriate evidence and sound argument. It will enable you to consolidate your knowledge and understanding of your surroundings, and will also help you to hold your own in a discussion and to critically analyse the claims and arguments made by others.

PART I

RESEARCH THEORY AND PRACTICE

One reviewer of my initial draft of this book suggested that these first five chapters did not deal with research methods at all. Strictly speaking, if you take a purist's view of what research methods are, he was correct. If you consider that research methods are only specific techniques for collecting and analysing data in such a way that you can come to reliable conclusions, then Part I of this book does not deal with these. However, I believe that unless you know what research is about, and understand the context in which these research methods are used, you will not know which to use and why. Therefore, in Part I of this book, I have provided an overview of the nature of research, its theoretical foundations, what is involved in the process, what you can do with it and what makes good research.

In order to place research within its context, in Chapter 2 I have provided you with a brief review of the theoretical basis of research as an activity. I consider different ideas about what we can know and how we can know it, and how we can get an understanding of the world around us. You will see that this type of thinking has a long history, probably ever since humans became aware of themselves as being special within nature. The ability to reflect and use abstract ideas set them apart from the animal and plant kingdom. The debate revolves around the extent to which humans can be autonomous from their environment and society.

In Chapter 3, I look at how research projects are structured. Of course, not all projects are the same, but they do all share some similar features. For example, they all have some aims and an argument that leads to some conclusions based on evidence of some kind.

The ways that the aims can be formulated are described, and the way that arguments can be constructed are discussed.

The important issue of ethics is explored in Chapter 4. The reliability of progress in knowledge is dependent on the honesty of the researchers. It also often depends on the cooperation of members of the public or particular sections of the population, who must be protected from any adverse effects of the research process. Basically, the principle behind ethical research is to cause no harm and, if possible, to produce some gain for the participants in the project and in the wider world.

Any piece of research will not be the first of its kind. There is always a context in which the project is carried out and a history of work that has gone before it. In Chapter 5, I consider how to review the literature in relation to your chosen subject, where to find the information and how to assess what you have found in relation to your projected work. This is a basic scholarly exercise, but once you have learned the skills needed to interrogate the accumulated knowledge and theories of a subject, you will find that this is useful in many aspects of life, particularly as we are bombarded from all sides with claims and assertions.

RESEARCH BASICS

Research is a very general term for an activity that involves finding out, in a more-or-less systematic way, things you did not know. A more academic interpretation is that research involves finding out about things that no one else knew either. It is about advancing the frontiers of knowledge.

Research methods are the techniques you use to do research. They represent the tools of the trade, and provide you with ways to collect, sort and analyse information so that you can come to some conclusions. If you use the right sort of methods for your particular type of research then you should be able to convince other people that your conclusions have some **validity**, and that the new knowledge you have created is soundly based.

It would be really boring to learn about all these tools without being able to try them out – like reading about how to use a plane, chisel, drill, etc. and never using them to make something out of a piece of wood. Therefore courses in research methods are commonly linked to assignments that require these methods to be applied – an actual research project that is described in a dissertation or thesis, or a research report. In the workplace, it is often the other way around. When there is a perception that more information and understanding are needed to advance the work, or process of work, then ways are sought as to how research can be carried out to meet this need.

Being a researcher is as much about doing a practical job as being academically competent. Identifying a subject to research, finding and collecting information and analysing it, presents you with a range of practical problems that need to be solved. Over hundreds of years, techniques or methods have been evolved to provide solutions to these problems. The practice of research is closely bound up with the theoretical developments that were promoted by philosophers and key thinkers and practitioners in the sciences, right back to the ancient Greeks. The debate about knowledge and how we acquire it is rooted in philosophical thought (discussed in Chapter 2).

WHAT YOU CAN DO WITH RESEARCH

So how can we use research to gain this new knowledge? Some of the ways it can be used are to:

- **categorize** – this involves forming a **typology** of objects, events or concepts, i.e. a set of names or 'boxes' into which these can be sorted. This can be useful in explaining which 'things' belong together and how;
- **describe** – descriptive research relies on observation as a means of collecting data. It attempts to examine situations to establish what is the norm, i.e. what can be predicted to happen again under the same circumstances;
- **explain** – this is a descriptive type of research specifically designed to deal with complex issues. It aims to move beyond 'just getting the facts' to make sense of the myriad other elements involved, such as human, political, social, cultural and contextual;
- **evaluate** – this involves making judgements about the quality of objects or events. Quality can be measured either in an absolute sense or on a comparative basis. To be useful, the methods of evaluation must be relevant to the context and intentions of the research;
- **compare** – two or more contrasting cases can be examined to highlight differences and similarities between them, leading to a better understanding of phenomena;
- **correlate** – the relationships between two phenomena are investigated to see whether and how they influence each other. The relationship might be just a loose link at one extreme or a direct link when one phenomenon causes another. These are measured as levels of association;
- **predict** – this can sometimes be done in research areas where correlations are already known. **Predictions** of possible future

behaviours or events are made on the basis that if there has been a strong relationship between two or more characteristics or events in the past, then these should exist in similar circumstances in the future, leading to predictable outcomes;

- **control** – once you understand an event or situation, you may be able to find ways to control it. For this you need to know what the cause and effect relationships are and that you are capable of exerting control over the vital ingredients. All of technology relies on this ability to control.

You can combine two or more of these objectives in a research project, with sometimes one objective needing to be successfully achieved before starting the next. For example, you usually need to be able to explain how something happens before you can work out how to control it.

RESEARCH DESIGNS

There are numerous types of research design that are appropriate for the different types of research projects. The choice of which design to apply depends on the nature of the problems posed by the research aims. Each type of research design has a range of research methods that are commonly used to collect and analyse the type of **data** that are generated by the investigations. Here is a list of some of the more common research designs, with a short explanation of the characteristics of each.

Historical

This aims at a systematic and objective evaluation and synthesis of evidence in order to establish facts and draw conclusions about past events. It uses primary historical data, such as archaeological remains as well as documentary sources of the past. It is usually necessary to carry out tests to check the **authenticity** of these sources. Apart from informing us about what happened in previous times and re-evaluating beliefs about the past, historical research can be used to find contemporary solutions based on the past and to inform present and future trends. It stresses the importance of interactions and their effects.

Descriptive

This design relies on observation as a means of collecting data. It attempts to examine situations in order to establish what is the norm, i.e. what can be predicted to happen again under the same circumstances. 'Observation' can take many forms. Depending on the type of information sought, people can be interviewed, questionnaires distributed, visual records made, even sounds and smells recorded. It is important that the observations are written down or recorded in some way so that they can be subsequently analysed. The scale of the research is influenced by two major factors: the level of complexity of the survey and the scope or extent of the survey.

Correlation

This design is used to examine a relationship between two concepts. There are two broad classifications of relational statements: an association between two concepts – where there is some kind of influence of one on the other – and a causal relationship – where one causes changes to occur in the other. **Causal statements** describe what is sometimes called a 'cause and effect' relationship. The cause is referred to as the **independent variable**; the variable that is affected is referred to as the **dependent variable**.

The correlation between two concepts can either be none (no correlation); positive (where an increase in one results in an increase in the other, or decrease results in a decrease); or negative (where an increase in one results in a decrease in the other or vice versa). The degree of association is often measurable.

Comparative

This design is used to compare past and present or different parallel situations, particularly when the researcher has no control over events. It can examine situations at different scales, macro (international, national) or micro (community, individual). **Analogy** is used to identify similarities in order to predict results – assuming that if two events are similar in certain characteristics, they could well be similar in others too. In this way, comparative design is used to explore and test what conditions were necessary to cause certain events, so that it is possible, for example, to understand the likely effects of making certain decisions.

Experimental

Experimental research attempts to isolate and control every relevant condition that determines the events investigated and then observes the effects when the conditions are manipulated. At its simplest, changes are made to an independent variable and the effects are observed on a dependent variable – i.e. cause and effect. Although experiments can be done to explore a particular event, they usually require a hypothesis (prediction) to be formulated first to determine what variables are to be tested and how they can be controlled and measured. There are several **classes** of experiment – pre, true, quasi, etc. which are characterized by the amount of checking and control involved in the methods.

Simulation

Simulation involves devising a representation – in a small and simplified form (**model**) – of a system, which can be manipulated to gauge effects. It is similar to experimental design in respect of this manipulation, but it provides a more artificial environment in that it does work with original materials at the same scale. Models can be mathematical (number crunching in a computer) or physical, working with two- or three-dimensional materials. The performance of the model must be checked and calibrated against the real system to check that the results are reliable. Simulation enables theoretical – what if? – situations to be tested.

Evaluation

This descriptive type of research is specifically designed to deal with complex social issues. It aims to move beyond 'just getting the facts', by trying to make sense of the myriad human, political, social, cultural and contextual elements involved. There are a range of different approaches of evaluation models; for example, systems analysis – which is a holistic type of research looking at the complex interplay of many variables; and responsive evaluation – which entails a series of investigative steps to evaluate how responsive a programme is to all those taking part in it. A common purpose of evaluation research is to examine the working of projects from the point of view of levels of awareness, costs and benefits, cost-effectiveness, attainment of objectives and quality assurance. The results are generally used to prescribe changes to improve and develop the situation.

Action

Essentially, this is an 'on-the-spot' procedure, principally designed to deal with a specific problem found in a particular situation. There is no attempt made to separate the problem from its context in order to study it in isolation. What are thought to be useful changes are made and then constant monitoring and evaluation are carried out to see the effects of the changes. The conclusions from the findings are applied immediately, and further monitored to gauge their effectiveness. Action research depends mainly on observation and behavioural data. Because it is so bound up in a particular situation, it is difficult to generalize the results, i.e. to be confident that the action will be successful in another context.

Ethnological

Ethnological research focuses on people. In this approach, the researcher is interested in how the subjects of the research interpret their own behaviour rather than imposing a theory from outside. It takes place in the undisturbed natural settings of the subjects' environment. It regards the context to be equally important as the actions it studies, and attempts to represent the totality of the social, cultural and economic situation. This is not easy, as much of culture is hidden and rarely made explicit and the cultural background and assumptions of the researcher may unduly influence interpretations and descriptions. Moreover, confusion can be produced by the use of language and the different meanings which may be given to words by the respondents and the researcher.

Feminist

This is more of a perspective than a research design. It involves theory and analysis, which highlight the differences between men's and women's lives. Researchers who ignore these differences can come to incorrect conclusions. However, everyone is male or female, so value neutrality is impossible, as no researcher practises research outside his or her system of values. Specific methods are not seen to be particularly feminist, but the methodology used is informed by theories of gender relations. Although feminist research is undertaken with a political commitment to identify and transform gender relations, it is not uniquely political but exposes all methods of social research as being political.

Cultural

Many of the prevailing theoretical debates (e.g. postmodernism, post-structuralism, etc.) are concerned with the subjects of language and cultural interpretation. Cultural research provides methodologies that allow a consistent analysis of cultural texts so that they can be compared, replicated, disproved and generalized. Examples of approaches to the interpretation of cultural texts are: content analysis, semiotics and discourse analysis. The meaning of the term 'cultural texts' has been broadened from that of purely literary works to that of the many different forms of communication – both formal, such as opera, TV news programmes, cocktail parties, etc. and informal, such as how people dress or converse.

Arts-based

This growing branch of research uses narrative enquiry, fiction, poetry, music, dance and movement, theatre and dream, film and visual arts as vehicles for exploring and elucidating social and cultural phenomena. A particular strength of this methodology is the connections it can draw between individual lives and the contexts in which we live, enabling very personal forms of expression that can be addressed to the outside world. The arts can be seen to provide the means for a holistic process that melds purpose and method in a seamless relationship. The immediate, captivating and aesthetically powerful media of the arts are harnessed to communicate the emotional aspects of human life. They have the power to create critical awareness and can be used to challenge stereotypes – to portray multiple meanings as well as to promote effective participation between researchers and subjects.

DECIDING ON YOUR TYPE OF RESEARCH

It is your research interest that decides the nature of your research problem, and this will indicate the appropriate type of research to follow. Once the objectives of a research project have been established, the issue of how these objectives can be met leads to a consideration of which research design should be chosen. The research design provides a framework for the collection and analysis of data and subsequently indicates which research methods are appropriate. You can combine two or more types of research design, particularly when your subject combines the study of human behaviour with that of, for example, economics, technology, legislation or organizations.

The different types of research design may involve use of their own specific types of research methods, developed specifically to solve the problems inherent in that design. However, some methods are widely used across many research types.

TAKING PRIDE IN THE IMPORTANCE AND QUALITY OF YOUR WORK

Doing a personal research project is a brilliant way to demonstrate your skills and knowledge in a subject. But to do this effectively, it is important not only to enjoy the process of being motivated by your fascination with the issue that you have chosen to investigate, but also to take it seriously and use the time you have efficiently. This is why it is a good idea to study the contents of this book, which will help you to make informed decisions on the way, save time by avoiding wrong turnings and understand what good quality means in terms of your research. Your well-thought-out and executed project, which you have clearly described in your dissertation or thesis, will stand as valuable evidence of your highly developed skills and great personal character when you apply for jobs in the future.

WHERE TO FIND OUT MORE

Apart from continuing to read this book, there are other introductions to research that you may wish to check out. Most books on this subject cover the whole sequence of doing research. The following books are aimed at undergraduate and postgraduate research, and selective reading of the preliminary chapters will provide further guidance on research basics. Each gives a slightly different view of the issues, so refer to as many as possible. You can probably do this in the library without even taking the books out on loan.

Blaxter, L., Hughes, C. and Tight, M. (2010) *How to Research* (fourth edition). Buckingham: Open University Press.

The first chapter gives an entertaining review of what research is about.

Rudestam, K.E. and Newton, R. (2014) *Surviving Your Dissertation: A Comprehensive Guide to Content and Process* (fourth edition). Thousand Oaks, CA: Sage.

Again, the first couple of chapters provide an introduction to research.

David, M. and Sutton, C. (2004) *Social Research: The Basics*. London: Sage.

A good chapter on getting started.

Swetnam, D. (2000) *Writing Your Dissertation: How to Plan, Prepare and Present Successful Work* (third edition). Oxford: How To Books.

Chapter 1 gives some simple advice on how to get started.

Biggam, J. (2008) *Succeeding with Your Master's Dissertation: A Step-by-Step Handbook*. Basingstoke: Palgrave.

A useful, simple and easy-to-read book for a person that has not done a dissertation before.

2

RESEARCH THEORY

Research is about acquiring knowledge and developing understanding; collecting facts and interpreting them to build up a picture of the world around us, and even within us. It is fairly obvious, then, that we should hold a view on what knowledge is and how we can make sense of our surroundings. These views will be based on the philosophical stance that we take.

Despite this, some people maintain that a study of the philosophy of the natural or human sciences is irrelevant to researchers. They remark that the study of philosophy consists of learning about how theory after theory has been erected, only to be torn down by the subsequent one, and that it has little bearing on the day-to-day practice of research and only causes confusion. So why should you find it necessary to know something about philosophy as a background to your research? Because everyone is a philosopher – everyone has a concept of the world. In fact, the alternative to having a philosophy is not having no philosophy but having a bad philosophy. The 'unphilosophical' person has an unconscious philosophy, which they apply in their practice – whether of science or politics or daily life (Collier, 1994: 16).

All philosophical positions and their attendant methodologies, explicitly or implicitly, hold a view about reality. This view, in turn, will determine what can be regarded as legitimate knowledge. Philosophy works by making arguments explicit. You need to develop sensitivity towards philosophical issues so that you can evaluate research critically. It will help you to discern the underlying, and perhaps contentious, assumptions upon which research reports are based even when these are not explicit, and thus enable you to judge the appropriateness of the methods that have been employed and the validity of the conclusions reached. Obviously, you will also have to consider these aspects with regard to your own research work. Your research, and how you carry it out, is deeply influenced by the theory or philosophy that underpins it.

There are different ways of going about doing research depending on your assumptions about what actually exists in reality; what we can know (metaphysics); and how we can acquire knowledge (epistemology).

METAPHYSICS AND EPISTEMOLOGY

Metaphysics is concerned with questions such as:

- What is it to be?
- Who are we?
- What is knowledge?
- What are things?
- What is time and space?

At one extreme is:

- **idealism** – which advocates that reality is all in the mind; that everything that exists is in some way dependent on the activity of the mind. Hence, as phenomena are reliant on mental and social factors they are therefore in a state of constant change – e.g. music is not just sound, it is an emotional experience;

and at the other extreme is:

- **materialism (or reductionism)** – which insists that only physical things and their interactions exist and that our minds and consciousness are wholly due to the active operation of materials. Hence, phenomena are independent of social factors and are therefore stable – e.g. music is just vibrations in the air.

As you can imagine, these are opposite ends of a spectrum, with many intermediate positions being held that balance the importance of the mind and material things in different degrees.

Epistemology is the theory of knowledge, especially regarding its validation and the methods used. It deals with how we know things and what we can regard as acceptable knowledge in a discipline.

It is concerned with the reliability of our senses and the power of the mind. As for the methods of acquiring knowledge, there are two basic approaches:

1   **empiricism** – knowledge gained by sensory experience (using inductive reasoning);
2   **rationalism** – knowledge gained by reasoning (using deductive reasoning).

The relative merits of these approaches have been argued ever since the ancient Greeks – Aristotle advocating the first and Plato the second.

INDUCTIVE AND DEDUCTIVE REASONING

The kinds of reasoning behind the empirical and rationalist approaches to gaining knowledge also start from opposite ends of a spectrum. Although it is not possible to apply either extreme in a practical way, it is useful to characterize the distinct differences in the two opposing approaches. A more practical approach that goes a long way to overcome the shortcomings of each is the **hypothetico-deductive method**, which uses the features of each in a pragmatic way. In fact, this method is used in much scientific enquiry and, hence, is also called the **scientific method**.

Inductive reasoning – the empiricist's approach

Inductive **reasoning** starts from specific observations or sensory experiences and then develops a general conclusion from them. This simple example gives an indication of the line of reasoning:

All the giraffes that I have seen have very long necks.	(Repeated observations)
Therefore, I conclude that all giraffes have long necks.	(Conclusion)

Induction is the earliest and, even now, the commonest popular form of scientific activity. We use it every day in our normal lives as we learn from our surroundings and experiences. We come to conclusions from what we have experienced and then generalize from them, that is, set them up as a rule or belief. The Elizabethan philosopher Francis Bacon stated that one should consult nature, and not rely on the writings of ancient philosophers such as Aristotle or on the Bible. The scientific revolution in the seventeenth century was based on this approach, led by such scientists as Galileo and Newton (remember the apple that fell on his head from the tree which led to his theory of gravity? Nice story anyway!). Mendel's discovery of genetics and Darwin's theory of evolution are perhaps the most famous generalizations in the form of theories that are, even by them, claimed to be developed through inductive reasoning.

However, there are problems with induction. First, how many observations must be made before we can reasonably draw a conclusion that is reliable enough to generalize from? Second, in how many situations and under which conditions should observations be made so that true conclusions can be reached? These problems do not stop us from using inductive reasoning every day quite successfully without even thinking about it. But we should be aware that what might at first seem obvious may not be so reliable on making further investigations.

Therefore, in order to be able to rely on the conclusions we come to by using inductive reasoning, we should ensure that we make a large number of observations; that we repeat them under a large range of circumstances and conditions; and that no observations contradict the generalization we have made from the repeated observations.

In the social sciences, research based on this approach is referred to as **grounded theory**, which uses collected data to develop a theory rather than to test or refine an existing one. The main emphasis is on a continuous data collection process interlaced with periodic pauses for analysis. The analysis is used to tease out categories in the data on which the subsequent data collection can be based. This reciprocal procedure is continued until these categories are 'saturated', i.e. the new data no longer provide new evidence. From these results, concepts and theoretical frameworks can be developed. This gradual emergence and refinement of theory based on observations is the basis for the 'grounded' label of this approach.

Deductive reasoning – the rationalist's approach

Deductive reasoning begins with general statements (premises) and, through logical argument, comes to a specific conclusion. Again, a simple example will provide a guide to how this works:

All living things will eventually die.	(General statement – first premise)
This animal is a living thing.	(Inference – second premise)
Therefore, this animal will eventually die.	(Conclusion)

This is the simplest form of deductive argument, and is called a syllogism. As you can see it consists of a general statement (called the first premise), followed by a more specific statement inferred from this (the second premise), and then a conclusion which follows on logically from the two statements

Deduction, as with many philosophical ideas, was first discussed as a way of reasoning by the ancient Greeks, in particular Plato. Enquiry is guided by the theory which precedes it. Theories are speculative answers to perceived problems, and they are tested by observation and experiment. While it is possible to confirm the possible truth of a theory through observations that support it, theory can be falsified and totally rejected by making observations that are inconsistent with its statement. In this way, science is seen to proceed by trial and error: when one theory is rejected another is proposed and tested, and thus the fittest theory survives.

In order for a theory to be tested, it must be expressed as a statement called a **hypothesis**. The essential nature of a hypothesis is that it must be falsifiable. This means that it must be logically possible to make true observational statements which conflict with the hypothesis, and thus can falsify it. However, the process of **falsification** leads to a devastating result of total rejection of a theory, requiring a completely new start.

Another problem with deductive reasoning is that the truth of the conclusions depends very much on the truth of the premise on which they are based. For example, in the past many conclusions about the movement of the planets were incorrect due to the premise that the earth was the centre of the universe.

Hypothetico-deductive reasoning or scientific method

The hypothetico-deductive method combines inductive and deductive reasoning, resulting in the to-and-fro process of:

- identification or clarification of a problem
- developing a hypothesis (testable theory) inductively from observations
- charting their implications by deduction
- practical or theoretical testing of the hypothesis
- rejecting or refining it in the light of the results.

It is this combination of experience with deductive and inductive reasoning that is the foundation of modern scientific research, commonly referred to as scientific method. It was only by the beginning of the 1960s that Popper (1902–92) formulated the idea of the hypothetico-deductive method, even though it must have already been used in practice for decades.

Of course, there are many problems posed by the complexity of testing theories in real life. Realistic scientific theories consist of a combination of statements, each of which relies on assumptions based on previous theories. The methods of testing are likewise based on assumptions and influenced by surrounding conditions. If the predictions of the theory are not borne out in the results of the tests, it could be the underlying premises which are at fault rather than the theory itself.

There are certain assumptions that underlie scientific method that relate to a materialist view of metaphysics and a positivist view of epistemology. These assumptions are:

- **order** – the universe is an ordered system that can be investigated and the underlying 'rules' can be exposed;
- **external reality** – we all share the same reality that does not depend on our existence. We can therefore all equally contribute to and share knowledge that reflects this reality;
- **reliability** – we can rely on our senses and reasoning to produce facts that reliably interpret reality;

- **parsimony** – the simpler the explanation the better. Theories should be refined to the most compact formulation;
- **generality** – the 'rules' of reality discovered through research can be applied in all relevant situations, regardless of time and place.

However, these assumptions are not accepted by the opposite camp in metaphysics and epistemology. Those with an idealist and relativist point of view insist on the importance of human subjectivity and the social dimension to facts and their meanings. This clash of view-points is unlikely ever to be resolved.

A brief review of history will show that this quest for what is reality and what are facts is a constant preoccupation in the enquiry into our relation to existence.

POSITIVISM, RELATIVISM, POSTMODERNISM AND CRITICAL REALISM

There is an important issue that confronts the study of the social sciences that is not so pertinent in the natural sciences. This is the question of the position of the human subject and researcher, and the status of social phenomena. Is human society subject to **laws** that exist independently of the human actors that make up society, or do individuals and groups create their own versions of social forces? As briefly mentioned above, the two extremes of approach are termed **positivism** and **interpretivism**. Again, as in the case of ways of reasoning, a middle way has also been formulated that draws on the useful characteristics of both approaches.

Positivism

The positivist approach to scientific investigation is based on acceptance as fact that the world around us is real, and that we can find out about these realities. There is an order made up of atomistic, discrete and observable events. Knowledge is derived using scientific method and based on sensory experience gained through experiments or comparative analysis. It aims at developing a unique and elegant description of any chosen aspect of the world that is true, regardless of what people think. By developing these scientific facts, knowledge is built up in a cumulative fashion, despite some false starts. Science builds on what is already known, for example, even Einstein's radical theories are a development from Newton's.

The approach to knowledge is reductionist in character, by maintaining that less measurable sciences are reducible to more measurable ones. Sociology is reducible to psychology, psychology to biology, biology to chemistry, and chemistry to physics. Social sciences can therefore be value free and objective.

Relativism (also called interpretivism, idealism, constructivism or even constructionism)

The alternative approach to research – **relativism** – is based on the philosophical doctrines of idealism and humanism. It maintains that the view of the world we see around us is the creation of the mind. This does not mean that the world is not real, but rather that we can only experience it personally through our perceptions which are influenced by our preconceptions, beliefs and values; we are not neutral, disembodied observers but part of society. Unlike the natural sciences, the researcher is not observing phenomena from outside the system, but is inextricably bound into the human situation that he/she is studying. As well as concentrating on the search for constants in human behaviour, which highlights the repetitive, predictable and invariant aspect of society, the researcher does not ignore what is subjective, individual and creative – facts and values cannot be separated. The researcher encounters a world already interpreted, and his/her job is to reveal this according to the meanings created by humans rather than to discover universal laws. Therefore, there can be more than one perspective and interpretation of a phenomenon.

Table 2.1 compares the alternative bases for interpreting the world. Just because the differences of perspective between positivist and relativist approaches are so radical, don't think that you need to espouse purely one or the other approach. Different aspects of life lend themselves to different methods of interpretation.

Postmodernism

Postmodernism challenges key issues such as meaning, knowledge and truth, which has opened up new perspectives and ideas about the essence of research. It denounces the meta-narratives

Table 2.1 Comparison between positivist and relativist approaches

Issue	Positivist	Relativist
Philosophical basis	Realism: the world exists and is knowable as it really is.	Idealism: the world exists but different people construe it in very different ways.
The role of research	To discover universal laws and generalizations.	To reveal different interpretations of the world as made by people.
Role of researcher	Neutral observer.	Part of the research process.
Theoretical approach	Rational, using inductive and scientific methods and value-free data.	Subjective, using inductive methods and value-laden data.
Methods	Experiments or mathematical models and quantitative analysis to validate, reject or refine hypotheses.	Surveys and observations with qualitative analysis to seek meaningful relationships and the consequences of their interactions. Analysis of language and meaning.
Analysis of society	Search for order. Society is governed by a uniform set of values and made possible only by acceptance of these values.	Search for dynamics. Multitude of values leading to complex interactions. Society made possible by negotiation.

(all-embracing theories) of the modern movement as a product of the Enlightenment, and insists on the inseparable links between knowledge and power. In fact, there is no universal knowledge or truth. Science is just a construct and only one of many types of knowledge that are all subjects of continual reinvention and change.

It is a complex combination of ideas that emerged in a fragmented fashion at the end of the nineteenth century but became highly developed by French social theorists such as Barthes, Derrida, Foucault, Baudrillard and Lyotard in the latter part of the twentieth century.

One of the strands of postmodernism examines the structure of language and how it is used. It challenges the assumption that language can be precisely used to represent reality. Meanings of words are ambiguous, as words are only signs or labels given to concepts (what is signified) and therefore there is no necessary correspondence between the word and the meaning, the signifier and the signified. The use of signs (words) and their meanings can vary depending on the flow of the text in which they are used, leading to the possibility of 'deconstructing' text to reveal its underlying inconsistencies. This approach can be applied to all forms of representation – pictures, films, etc. that gain added or alternative meanings by the overlaying of references to previous uses. This can be seen particularly in the media, where it is difficult to distinguish the real from the unreal – everything is representation, there is no reality.

In another strand of postmodernism, Foucault maintained that representations of knowledge are developed through types of discourse – discussions that are framed by the current accepted norms of institutions that are in positions of power within the intellectual establishment, such as universities, government bodies and funding institutions. In this way, scientific enquiry and the application of the knowledge gained by it, rather than being freely conducted, are channelled towards supporting the interests of these institutions. Science is now a sort of game bound up with money, power and technology instead of being a simple search for truths.

These attitudes imply that the grand, monolithic structure of science and knowledge built up over the centuries, the striving after facts and laws that represent universal truths, and the steady progress towards greater understanding of the world and control of it through technology, is an impossible mission. Enquiry must be broken down into much smaller, localized and limited explanations, stressing different influences, ideologies and identities and the overwhelming complexity of our existence. There can be no overarching theories and no universal truths – all is relative (see Table 2.2).

Critical realism

Inevitably, there has been a reaction to this postmodernist challenge to traditional science which threatens a descent into chaos and powerlessness to act because of the lack of possibility of agreement on truths and reality. This has been labelled **critical realism** and it is based on critical reasoning.

Critical reasoning can be seen as a reconciliatory approach, which recognizes, like the positivists, the existence of a natural order in

Table 2.2 Methods of enquiry – a comparison

Basic beliefs	Positivism/ post-positivism	Relativism/ interpretivism	Postmodernism/ emancipatory
Metaphysics (nature of reality)	One reality; knowable within probability	Multiple, socially constructed realities	Multiple realities shaped by social, political, cultural, economic, ethnic, gender and disability values
Epistemology (nature of knowledge; relation between knower and would-be-known)	Objectivity is important; researcher manipulates and observes in dispassionate, objective manner	Interactive link between researcher and participants; values are made explicit; creating findings	Interactive link between researcher and participants; knowledge is socially and historically situated

Source: Adapted from Mertens (1998: 9).

social events and discourse, but claims that this order cannot be detected by merely observing a pattern of events. The underlying order must be discovered through the process of **interpretation** while doing theoretical and practical work, particularly in the social sciences. Unlike the positivists, critical realists do not claim that there is a direct link between the concepts they develop and the observable phenomena. Concepts and theories about social events are developed on the basis of their observable effects, and interpreted in such a way that they can be understood and acted upon, even if the interpretation is open to revision as understanding grows. This also distinguishes critical realists from relativists, who deny the existence of such general structures divorced from the specific event or situation and the context of the research and researcher.

SO MUCH FOR THEORY, WHAT ABOUT APPLICATION?

It's all very well for me to explain the different ways of thinking and their historical roots, but how will this apply to your own research project? First, your awareness of the different philosophical approaches should raise the questions in your mind: what way do I think about my investigations? What sort of approach is commonly used in this subject?

To answer these, you need to read and analyse the literature on research in your area of study to discover the assumptions and philosophical approaches that are commonly used. Apart from the mainstream, there will certainly be mavericks or original thinkers who take a different stance and challenge the received knowledge. Then you need to consider your own approach to thinking about it:

- Will you be starting out with an assumption or statement of fact (a hypothesis) and use your research to test whether it stands up to scrutiny (testing the hypothesis to see whether it is supported or refuted)? This will entail deductive reasoning.
- Will you be exploring a situation to find patterns or systems that explain the workings of the phenomenon under investigation? This will entail inductive reasoning.
- Are you looking for incontrovertible facts that you can establish that are independent of human influence or interpretation? A positivist approach.
- Are you seeking some understanding of a complicated human situation that will shed some light on the motivations, barriers, feelings and beliefs involved, perhaps to suggest ways of improvement or change? A relativist approach.
- Will you take a multi-perspective approach that seeks out physical facts where possible as well as delving into the subjective social issues involved which might help to explain why the facts are as they are? You will then be taking an emancipatory or critical realist approach.

To illustrate the way that research students have explained their approaches to their research, here are two examples with extracts from PhD theses. The first extract explains how research uses both a deductive and an inductive process, and the second considers the effect that different philosophical approaches have on the meaning of a concept and how this impacts on a particular situation today.

Research approach

The research strategy fulfilled the following requirements in order to answer the research question:

a) *Collect primary empirical data from people in England using the indicators from the conceptual framework to form hypotheses,*
b) *follow a deductive approach by collecting and analysing data that can be used to accept or reject hypotheses,*
c) *follow an inductive approach by collecting and analysing data that can be used to develop new hypotheses to address the research question.*

These requirements fit within a sequential explanatory mixed methods (quantitative and qualitative) research design strategy. Sequential explanatory mixed methods was used to corroborate findings in the study. The quantitative data (from a questionnaire) was collected and analysed first in order to test hypotheses developed from findings in the literature review (Phase 1). The findings from this analysis were used to collect qualitative data (from interviews) (Phase 2), which helped underpin the findings and generated further theory that was not highlighted by the quantitative study. This strategy helped overcome the weaknesses of quantitative data analysis using the strengths of qualitative analysis. In the case of this research, the weakness of the quantitative analysis was that all the questions asked were generated from presumed indicators from the literature review. The qualitative data brought forward new indicators that were not highlighted by the literature.

Source: Mina Samangooei

Research approach

The first part of the thesis undertakes a historical review of the changing roles of the ideas of the 'whole' and 'part' in urban thought and examines the different meanings and connotations of the term fragmentation in urban discourse. In particular the focus is set on the key role that fragmentation plays in two of the most important debates of the last three decades: postmodernism and globalisation. In the context of postmodernism, fragmentation generally has a celebratory connotation that is associated with liberation from 'modernist totalitarianism'. Within the framework of the debate on globalisation, fragmentation is commonly understood as a consequence of globalisation processes and their intrinsic 'integration–fragmentation' dynamics. In this sense fragmentation is either regarded as a problematic outcome of globalisation or as an indistinct characteristic of the new urban configurations in the global age.

The second part of the thesis narrows down the discussion, focusing on the case of Buenos Aires. The conceptual background developed in the first part is used to assess the role of urban and political-economic discourses on recent urban transformations; to determine whether and in what sense urban fragmentation has increased since the mid-1970s; and to conceptualise the case of the recent transformation of Abasto. The research approach undertaken proceeds from the most general to the most particular: from a review of the meanings of the term fragmentation in mainstream urban discourse worldwide, to the analysis of the meanings of urban fragmentation in the specific case of Buenos Aires, the local characterisation of fragmentation as a spatial phenomenon at different scales and the comprehensive examination of a single micro-urban case.

Source: Daniel Kozack

WHERE TO FIND OUT MORE

There is much written about the philosophy of knowledge and research, and it is advisable to have a good general knowledge of the debate about the philosophy of scientific knowledge and its detractors in order to place your research within the philosophical context. When compiling this chapter, I found the following books useful and well worth a browse. The titles give an indication of the subject tackled. I have put the more approachable ones first.

Two good introductory books to start with:

Thompson, M. (2006) *Philosophy*. London: Hodder (Teach Yourself).
This is a simple introduction to philosophy which explains the main terminology and outlines the principal streams of thought.

Warburton, N. (2012) *Philosophy: The Basics* (fifth edition). London: Routledge.
A book in the same series as this one. Gently eases you into the world of philosophy. Each chapter considers a key area of philosophy, explaining and exploring the basic ideas and themes.

The following concentrate on scientific approaches and dilemmas:

Benton, T. and Craib, I. (2010) *Philosophy of Social Science: The Philosophical Foundations of Social Thought* (second edition). Basingstoke: Palgrave Macmillan. This addresses critical issues relating to the nature of social science by interrogating the relationship between social science and natural science, and by encompassing traditional and contemporary perspectives introduces and critiques a wide range of approaches, from empiricism and positivism to post-structuralism and rationalism.

Chalmers, A. (2013) *What Is This Thing Called Science?* (fourth edition). Milton Keynes: Open University Press.
Now well into its fourth decade, this book has become something of a classic the world over. A refreshingly lucid introduction that draws on illuminating historical examples, asking and answering some of the most fundamental questions about the nature of science and its methods.

Hughes, J. (1997) *The Philosophy of Social Research* (third edition). Harlow: Longman.
This book introduces some of the important philosophical issues arising from social research practices and historical research in the social sciences.

Okasha, S. (2002) *Philosophy of Science: A Very Short Introduction*. Oxford: Oxford University Press.
A clear, non-technical introduction to the philosophy of science and social research.

And three influential books for the enthusiast!

Feyerabend, P. (1993) *Against Method: Outline of an Anarchistic Theory of Knowledge* (third edition). London: Verso.
Kuhn, T.S. (1970) *The Structure of Scientific Revolutions* (second edition). Chicago: Chicago University Press.
Popper, K. (1992) *The Logic of Scientific Discovery*. Routledge Classics. London: Routledge.

3

STRUCTURING THE RESEARCH PROJECT

Research projects are set up to explain a phenomenon or to test a theory. Research methods are the practical techniques used to carry out research. They are the 'tools of the trade' that make it possible to collect information and to analyse it. What information you collect and how you analyse it depends on the nature of the **research problem** – the central generating point of a research project. Hence the need for total clarity in defining the problem and limiting its scope in order to enable a practical research project with defined outcomes to be devised.

Mostly, research methods courses at undergraduate and more advanced levels culminate not in an exam, but in a research project or dissertation where you can demonstrate how you have understood the process of research and how various research methods are applied. Hence the need to be clear about the whole process, so that the methods can be seen within the context of a project.

THE RESEARCH PROCESS

It is necessary to first define a research problem in order to provide a reason for doing the research. The problem will generate the subject of the research, its aims and objectives. It will also indicate what data need to be collected to investigate the issues raised and what kind of analysis is suitable to enable you to come to conclusions, providing answers to the research questions raised by the problem.

This process is common to virtually all research projects, whatever their size and complexity. And they can be very different. These differences are due to their subject matter; for example, compare an investigation into sub-nuclear particles with a study of different teaching methods, differences in scales of time and resources, and extent of pioneering qualities and rigour. Some projects are aimed at testing and refining existing knowledge, others at creating new knowledge.

The answers to four important questions underpin the framework of any research project:

1   What are you going to do? The subject of your research.
2   Why are you going to do it? The reason for this research being necessary or interesting.
3   How are you going to do it? The research methods that you will use to carry out the project.
4   When are you going to do it? The programme of work.

The answers to these questions are not simple, but they will provide a framework for conducting the research. This book has been written to give you an indication of what is involved in answering these questions.

Figure 3.1 shows the structure of a typical research project. It shows a rather linear sequence of tasks, which is far tidier than what happens in reality. As knowledge and understanding increase during the

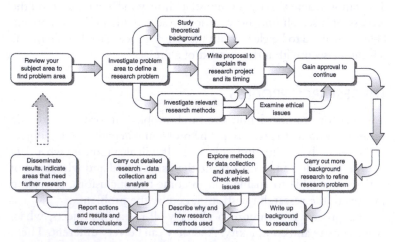

Figure 3.1 Structure of a typical research project

course of the project, it is subject to constant reiteration. However, a diagram is useful to explain the main order of different stages in the research, and it can be used to plan a timetabled programme of work. The progress of the project can then be gauged by comparing the current stage of work with the steps in the process.

THE RESEARCH PROBLEM

There is no shortage of problems throughout the world, but for a problem to be researchable, it needs to have several crucial features. It must be:

- stated clearly and concisely
- significant, i.e. not trivial or a repetition of previous work
- delineated, in order to limit its scope to practical investigation
- possible to obtain the information required to explore the problem
- possible to draw conclusions related to the problem, as the point of research is to find some answers.

A research problem can be based on a question, an unresolved controversy, a gap in knowledge or an unrequited need within the chosen subject. An awareness of current issues in the subject, an inquisitive and questioning mind, and an ability to express yourself clearly are required in order to find and formulate a problem that is suitable for a research project.

Initially, it is useful to define no more than a problem area within the general body of knowledge surrounding a subject, rather than a specific research problem, e.g. school truancy, energy saving in buildings, homecare for the elderly, etc. Then, by examining the different aspects of the problem area, you can home in on an aspect that is of interest to you, is controversial, or is of particular significance. Then a rationale for the research problem can be defined. This can be done, for example, by raising a question, defining some research objectives or formulating a hypothesis.

DEFINING THE RESEARCH PROBLEM

Here are several forms in which the research problem can be expressed to indicate the method of investigation.

Question or questions

Probably the simplest way to set up a research problem is to ask a question. This might be quite abstract in nature, so will require to be broken down into several sub-questions that can be practically investigated. The nice thing about questions is that they demand answers – a good incentive to do some research! Here is an example of a research problem expressed as a main question:

> Main question: Are school exam results a true test of a student's intelligence?

Questions can then be used to break the main problem down into further questions that define sub-problems. The different things you can do to split up the main question are to:

- split it down into different aspects that can be investigated separately, e.g. political, economic, cultural, technical;
- explore different personal or group perspectives, e.g. employers, employees;
- investigate different concepts used, e.g. health, wealth, confidence, sustainability;
- consider the question at different scales, e.g. the individual, group, organization;
- compare the outcomes of different aspects from the above ways of splitting down.

In this case, the sub-questions could concentrate on:

- What constitutes intelligence? (Investigating a concept – i.e. 'intelligence'.)
- What ways of testing intelligence are there? (Exploring different perspectives – i.e. other intelligence tests, and thus investigating the concept 'test'.)
- What sort of school exams are there and how are they marked? (Investigating another concept – i.e. 'exams'.)
- How do school exam criteria match those of the criteria of other intelligence tests? (Split into aspects – in this case, criteria of exams and other intelligence tests.)

Note how all the sub-questions relate directly to the main, rather abstract, question; they break it down into practical areas that can be investigated individually and built up to provide an answer to the main question. For smaller-scale studies, an exploratory approach may be used. The subject and scope of the exploration can be expressed in a statement of intent. Again, this must be derived from the research problem, imply a method of approach and indicate the outcome. An example of this form of research definition is:

> This study examines the problem of the career development of women engineers in the automotive industry in Britain. It focuses on the identification of specific barriers (established conventions, prejudices, procedures, career paths) and explores the effectiveness of specific initiatives that have been aimed at breaking down these barriers.

Note how the problem, in this case of career development, is narrowly delimited in order to put a boundary around the scope of the work, for example only women engineers, only in the automotive industry, and only in Britain. It also lists the practical tasks to be carried out, i.e. the identification of specific barriers and the exploration of initiatives. This list of barriers stipulates in more detail the actual subjects of the investigation.

Hypotheses

The research problem in projects that use the hypothetico-deductive method is expressed in terms of the testing of a particular hypothesis.

Hypotheses are nothing unusual; we make them all the time. If something happens in our everyday life, we tend to suggest a reason for its occurrence by making rational guesses. These reasonable guesses can be expressed in the form of a **statement**. This is a hypothesis. If, on further examination, a particular hypothesis is found to be supported, i.e. the reasons for its occurrence seem to be correct, we have a good chance that we can predict what will happen in the same situation in the future, or can devise actions to prevent it happening again. If the investigation shows that the guess was wrong, then it can be rejected as false. Many of the greatest discoveries in science were based on hypotheses: Newton's theory of gravity, Einstein's general theory of relativity and a host of others.

A good hypothesis is a very useful aid to organizing the research effort, but it must have certain qualities. It must be a statement that can be put to the test. It must specifically limit the enquiry to the interaction of certain factors (usually called variables) and suggest the methods appropriate for collecting, analysing and interpreting the data, and the resultant confirmation or rejection of the hypothesis through empirical or experimental testing must give a clear indication of the extent of knowledge gained.

So, to express the above example of a research question in the form of a hypothesis it would be written as a simple statement, like this:

> School exam results are a true test of a student's intelligence.

The formulation of the hypothesis is usually made on an abstract or conceptual level, to enable the results of the research to be generalized beyond the specific conditions of the study. However, one of the fundamental criteria of a hypothesis, that it is testable but formulated on a conceptual level, cannot be directly tested; it is too abstract. It is therefore necessary to convert it to an operational level. This is called **operationalization**.

Often, the first step is to break down the main hypothesis into two or more sub-hypotheses. These represent components or aspects of the main hypothesis and, together, should add up to its totality. Each sub-hypothesis will intimate a different method of testing and therefore implies different research methods that might be appropriate. This is a similar process to breaking down main research questions into sub-questions. For example:

> The intelligence of students can be measured.
>
> Tests have been devised to accurately measure levels of intelligence. School exams contain suitable tests to measure students' intelligence. The accuracy of school exams to test intelligence is commensurate with specially devised intelligence tests.

The operationalization of the sub-hypotheses follows four steps in the progression from the most abstract to the most concrete expressions by defining concepts, indicators, variables and values. These are described in more detail in Chapter 6.

Propositions

Focusing a research study on a set of **propositions**, rather than on a hypothesis, allows the study to concentrate on relationships between events, without having to comply with the rigorous characteristics required of hypotheses. The first proposition is a statement of a situation, which is then followed with further propositions that point out factors or events that are related to it and ends with one that indicates a conclusion that could be drawn from these interrelationships. An example will help explain this.

The main research problem was formulated in the form of three interrelated propositions:

- Specifically designed public sector housing provided for disabled people continues to be designed according to the government recommendations and standards for disabled people's housing.
- The recommendations and standards are not based on an accurate perception of the needs of disabled people.
- Therefore, there is a mismatch between the specifically designed public sector housing provided for disabled people and their accommodation requirements.

In this example, it is clear that the research must investigate what the actual accommodation requirements of disabled people are, what the government perception of their needs is, and how they compare.

THE USE OF ARGUMENT

The whole point of doing a research project is to identify a particular question or problem, to collect information and to present some answers or solutions. In order to convince the reader that you have collected information relevant to the question or problem and that you have based your answers and conclusions on the correct analysis of this information, you will need to use some logical **argument**.

You might want to defend or challenge a particular point of view or propose a new or improved one. You will have to play the part of a detective making a case in court. The detective will set out to solve the problem (who committed the crime and how?) by analysing the situation (the scene and events of the crime, the possible suspects), collecting and reviewing the evidence, then making a case for his/her conclusions about 'whodunit' and how. The jury will have to decide that the argument is convincing and that the evidence is sufficiently strong. In the case of a research project, you will be setting the problem and laying out your case, and the reader of your report, dissertation or thesis will be your jury.

As mentioned in the previous chapter, there are two basic stages to an argument: the **premises**, which are statements in the form of propositions or assertions that form the basis of the argument (this can be seen as the evidence) and the **conclusion**, which is a proposition that expresses the inference drawn by logical steps from the original premises.

Arguments are based on logical reasoning of which, as explained in the previous chapter, there are two basic types: inductive reasoning, which entails moving from repeated observations to a general conclusion, and deductive reasoning, which entails going from a general principle (called a premise) to a conclusion about a particular case. The hypothetico–deductive method, or scientific method, is a further development of logical reasoning based on the principle that we can never be completely sure of any premises or conclusions that we make, but we can be more confident about some than others. The more a premise or conclusion has been tested and supported by repeated investigations, the more likely it is to be true. Also, conclusions can be refined if they are only seen to be true in particular situations. All scientific facts, such as the theory of gravity, are based on this approach.

It is important to be aware of the type of reasoning that you will use to make your argument, or, if you are reading through the research literature, what type of reasoning is used by each of the writers. Of course, it is not always easy to detect the simple steps of the argument as described above, so it is worth knowing what to look out for when doing your background reading. There are also pitfalls that can occur to weaken or even invalidate the value of an argument, however persuasive it might seem at first reading.

Recognizing and testing arguments

As well as constructing arguments to support your research conclusions, it is also necessary to recognize and scrutinize other people's arguments, particularly those on whose work you are basing your research.

Recognizing arguments

In many types of writing and other forms of discourse, e.g. conversation, TV programmes, speeches, etc. the argument may be poorly expressed or submerged within the content. In order to recognize when an argument is being made, look for words that indicate a premise such as:

- since
- because
- if
- assuming that
- given that, etc.

Then look for words that indicate that a conclusion follows, such as:

- therefore
- this proves that
- then
- consequently
- thus, etc.

Then look for any logical reasoning and evidence that is given to link the two.

Testing arguments

There are techniques which can be used to detect the valid from the fallacious arguments, i.e. those whose logic follows the correct rules and those whose logic does not. Fallacies fall into two main categories: formal and informal.

Formal fallacies are those where the logical structure underpinning the argument is faulty in some way. There are many ways that logical structures can be faulty, too many to consider here, but for one example consider the following simple argument:

No lawyers are criminals.

John is not a lawyer.

Therefore, John is a criminal.

This makes a hidden assumption that all people who are not lawyers are criminals. This is not one of the premises. If a first line was added that went 'All non-lawyers are criminals' then the logic of the argument and its conclusion would be sound, despite the preposterous premises. Just like with computer programs: rubbish in – rubbish out!

Informal fallacies also come in many guises. These are misleading – not so much because the logical steps are incorrect, but because they make false analogies, use emotional and misleading claims, and jump to unjustified conclusions on evidence that is skimpy, irrelevant or untrue. The following example makes false analogies:

The ship of government, like any ship, works best when there is a strong captain in charge of it. That is why government by dictatorship is more effective.

Is a ship sufficiently like a government to make this claim?

Constructing an argument

Although Bonnett provides a choice of six types of argument (2001: 9), I reckon that there are only two basic aims of argumentation. One is to argue for a statement by providing evidence that will support it. The other is to refute a statement by providing evidence that undermines it. Between these opposites can be a combination of the two, which entails a less black-and-white approach by arguing for a revision or refinement of the statement to get nearer to the truth, again based on the evidence presented. Another combination compares two – usually opposing – statements, and argues that one is right and the other is wrong.

To argue in support of a concluding statement, you need to demonstrate that the premises are true. This may not be straightforward, as truth is often difficult to pin down. Evidence in the form of data confirmation or agreement amongst experts will help to substantiate the strength of your claim. In research, evidence will often be new data generated by the project, so the reliability of sources and the methods of data collection must be clearly explained and justified. You then must employ a sound logical progression of steps to bring you to your conclusions. The conclusions must be based exclusively on the premises. If it is not possible to be absolutely certain that the conclusions are inevitable, you have the option to soften the concluding statement with conditions such as, 'it is likely that', 'it is probable that', etc.

To refute a concluding statement requires you to show that the conclusion is false or untrue. This can be done by challenging the logic of the argument, challenging the truth of evidence on which the argument is based, or questioning the relevance or completeness of the evidence. Another way to challenge an argument is to produce counter-examples that are deployed against either the premises and/or conclusions. This will undermine the universality of the argument, demonstrating that it does not hold in all cases. Alternatively, you might be able to demonstrate that the conclusions drawn will lead to absurdity if taken far enough.

Constructing an argument and coming to conclusions about a research project is a cumulative process. It is unlikely that the chosen problem is simple, with questions raised that can be answered with a simple yes or no. Even if they can, you will be required to describe why it is one or the other and make an argument to support your case. Normally, the problem is broken down into smaller components requiring separate investigations. Conclusions about these components will occur in various sections of the analysis part of the report or dissertation. Skill is then required to gather these up in the concluding section to fit them together into a 'mosaic' that will present the complete picture of the conclusion to the main problem.

WHERE TO FIND OUT MORE

You can quickly get into deep water on the subject of thinking and argument. I would recommend the volumes by Brink-Budgen or Bonnett to start with, and perhaps follow up the references in there if you want to find out more on specific issues. The other sources I have listed require you to have either a special interest or a chosen topic that focuses on aspects of these subjects.

Brink-Budgen, R. (2010) *Critical Thinking for Students: Learn the Skills of Critical Assessment and Effective Argument* (fourth edition). Oxford: How To Books. This has an associated website for the exchange of ideas, experiences, etc.

Bonnett, A. (2011) *How to Argue* (third edition). Harlow: Pearson Education.
Cottrel, S. (2011) *Critical Thinking Skills: Developing Effective Analysis and Argument* (Palgrave Study Skills). Basingstoke: Palgrave Macmillan.

If you really want to get into more depth about logic and argument these are reasonably approachable books, listed in order of easiest first:

Hodges, W. (2001) *Logic: An Introduction to Elementary Logic* (second edition). London: Penguin.
Salmon, M.H. (2013) *Introduction to Logic and Critical Thinking* (sixth edition). Belmont, CA: Wadsworth.
Gensler, H.J. (1989) *Logic: Analyzing and Appraising Arguments*. London: Prentice-Hall International.
Fisher, A. (2004) *The Logic of Real Arguments* (second edition). Cambridge: Cambridge University Press.

These are two amusing books about fallacy that might interest you:

Pirie, M. (2015) *How to Win Every Argument: The Use and Abuse of Logic* (second edition). London: Continuum.
Well-written and entertaining.

Thouless, R.H. and Thouless, C.R. (2011) *Straight and Crooked Thinking* (fifth edition). London: Hodder Education Books.
A classic book first published in 1930, but still entertaining and thought-provoking.

RESEARCH ETHICS

Research, however novel its discoveries, is only valuable if it is carried out honestly. We cannot trust the results of a research project if we suspect that the researchers have not acted with integrity. Although it might be easy enough to take short cuts or even to cheat, it really is not worth it. Not only will your research be discredited when you are found out, but you will suffer severe penalties and humiliation.

It is a simple matter to follow the clear guidelines in citation that will prevent you from being accused of passing off other people's work as your own – called plagiarism. In fact, to refer to, or quote, other people's work is considered a virtue and demonstrates that you have read widely about your subject and are knowledgeable about the most important people and their ideas.

Working with human participants in your research always raises **ethical** issues about how you treat them. People should be treated with respect, which has many implications for exactly how you deal with them before, during and after the research. Educational and professional organizations who oversee research projects have strict ethical guidelines that must be followed. However, the issues can become quite complicated, with no clear-cut solutions. It is therefore important that you consult with others, especially advisers appointed for that purpose.

Even if you are not using human participants in your research, there is still the question of honesty in the way you collect, analyse and interpret data. By explaining exactly how you arrived at your conclusions, you can avoid accusations of cover-ups or false reasoning.

There are two aspects of ethical issues in research:

1   the individual values of the researcher relating to honesty, frankness and personal integrity;
2   the researcher's treatment of other people involved in the research, relating to informed consent, confidentiality, anonymity and courtesy.

Although the principles underpinning ethical practice are fairly straightforward and easy to understand, their application can be quite difficult in certain situations. Not all decisions can be clear-cut in the realm of human relations.

ORGANIZATIONS AND ETHICS COMMITTEES

All organizations that are involved in research involving human participants have set up a code of practice for their researchers. To see typical examples of these types of guidelines, you can refer to the web page produced by the British Educational Research Association (www.bera.ac.uk/guidelines.htms) or the British Sociological Association statement of ethical practice (www.britsoc.co.uk/index). Universities will have their own codes of practice.

The role of ethics committees is to oversee the research carried out in their organizations in relation to ethical issues. It is they who formulate the research ethics code of conduct and monitor its application in the research carried out by members of their organizations. Applying for ethics approval inevitably involves filling in forms.

HONESTY IN YOUR WORK

Honesty is essential, not only to enable straightforward, above-board communication, but to engender a level of trust and credibility in the outcomes of the research. This applies to all researchers, no matter what subject they are investigating. Although honesty must be maintained in all aspects of the research work, it is worth focusing here on several of the most important issues.

Intellectual ownership and plagiarism

Unless otherwise stated, what you write will be regarded as your own work; the ideas will be considered your own unless you say to the contrary. The worst offence against honesty in this respect is called **plagiarism**: directly copying someone else's work into your report, thesis, etc. and letting it be assumed that it is your own. Using the thoughts, ideas and works of others without acknowledging their source, even if paraphrased into your own words, is unethical. Don't be tempted to copy and paste any text or illustrations from the internet or a publication, however obscure, without citing the source. Remember that the process of learning is dependent on exploring the ideas of others, the more the better, so there is no shame in using numerous sources. Indeed, you can thereby demonstrate your wide reading.

It is worth remembering that programs such as ProCite, which are used to detect plagiarism, are now extremely sophisticated and can detect even the most obscure sources, including other students' work. Equally serious is claiming sole authorship of work which is in fact the result of collaboration or amanuensis ('ghosting'). See the next section on how you can acknowledge other people's work through citation and referencing.

But there are instances where you will have to use your judgement about how you distinguish between your own ideas and those of others. There are many areas of common knowledge that are not attributable to any single source and cannot be claimed to be your own discovery. It is good practice to introduce such statements 'as is commonly acknowledged' or 'it is well-known fact', or similar. You will also have to judge, when you are using the ideas or work of others, the extent to which your writing is simply presenting these, whether by direct quotation or paraphrase, or making an appraisal or comparison of them. In the former case the ideas of others must be acknowledged, while your commentary upon them is of course your own work. This is actually the stuff of academic writing, particularly when presenting a literature review. If in doubt, cite!

Table 4.1 shows three main ways of avoiding plagiarism while still using material from other sources.

Table 4.1 Ways to avoid plagiarism

Technique	Form	Method	Citation
Quoting	Write exactly the same words as in the original.	Enclose the quotation in inverted commas (quotation marks) for short quotations. For longer quotations, insert as a paragraph inset on both sides, and consider using a different font.	Cite the author, date of publication and page number.
Paraphrasing	Include key points and sub-points from the original source.	Write a paraphrase in your own words and use your own sentence strucure. Use synonyms, change the word order, change numbers and percentages in different forms, convert from active voice to passive voice (or vice versa).	Cite the author and date of publication.
Summarizing	Shorten text by restating only the main ideas in as few words as possible. Either informative or descriptive in style.	Mention author and title in first sentence. In your own words explain the central idea and then the main concepts and points in the argument, together with conclusion. Omit minor details and examples.	Add the date of publication to complete citation.

Acknowledgement and citation

Obviously, in no field of research can you rely entirely on your own ideas, concepts and theories. You can avoid accusations of plagiarism by acknowledging the sources of these features and their originators within your own text. This is called **citation**. Although there are several well-established citation methods, they all consist of brief annotations or numbers placed within the text that identify the cited material, and a **list of references** at the end of the text that give the full publication details of the source material. These methods of reference cater for direct quotations or ideas, etc. from the work of others gathered from a wide variety of sources (such as books, journals, conferences, talks, interviews, TV programmes, etc.), and should be meticulously used. See the section on 'Where to find out more' for detailed instructions on the accepted methods of citation and reference. You should also indicate the assistance of others and any collaboration with others, usually in the form of a written acknowledgement at the beginning or end of the report.

Responsibility and accountability of the researcher

Apart from correct attribution, honesty is essential in the substance of what you write. You do have responsibilities to fellow researchers, respondents, the public and the academic community. Accurate descriptions are required of what you have done, how you have done it, the information you obtained, the techniques you used, the analysis you carried out, and the results of experiments – a myriad of details concerning every part of your work.

Data and interpretations

Although it is difficult, and some maintain that it is impossible, to be free from bias, distorting your data or results knowingly is a serious lapse of honesty. Scientific objectivity should be maintained as much as possible. If you can see any reason for a possibility of bias in any aspect of the research, it should be acknowledged and explained. If the study involves personal judgements and assessments, the basis for these should be given. Silently rejecting or ignoring evidence which happens to be contrary to one's beliefs, or being too selective in the data used and in presenting the results of the analysis, constitutes a breach of integrity.

The sources of financial support for the research activities should be mentioned, and pressure and sponsorship from sources that might influence the impartiality of the research outcomes should be avoided.

Where do you stand?

The theoretical perspective, or epistemology, of the researcher should be made clear at the outset of the research so that the 'ground rules' or assumptions that underpin the research can be understood by the readers and, in some instances, the subjects of the research. One of the principal functions of doing background research is to explore just this aspect, and to come to decisions on theory that will form the basis of your research approach. The theoretical approach will influence the type of data collection and analysis used. These methods are not ethically neutral, so they will raise ethical issues.

SITUATIONS THAT RAISE ETHICAL ISSUES

Social research, and other forms of research which study people and their relationships to each other and to the world, need to be particularly sensitive about issues of ethical behaviour. As this kind of research often impinges on the sensibilities and rights of other people, researchers must be aware of necessary ethical standards which should be observed to avoid any harm that might be caused by carrying out or publishing the results of the research project.

Research aims

Although research aimed merely at gaining greater knowledge and understanding of a phenomenon has few or no ethical consequences – the expansion of scientific knowledge is generally regarded as a good thing – applied research is more easily subjected to ethical investigation. Will the results of the research benefit society, or at least not harm it? Will there be losers as well as gainers? The research aims and their consequences must be clearly stated. Normally, you will have to argue that the aims of your research are in accordance with the ethical standards prescribed by your university or organization.

Use of language

How you use language has an important influence when conducting and writing up research. You should aim to be as neutral as possible in the way you use terminology involving people – who and what they are, and what they do. Guard against being patronizing or disparaging, and avoid bias, stereotyping, discrimination, prejudice, intolerance and discrimination. You will notice that acceptable terminology changes with time, so be aware that terms used in some older literature are not suitable for use now. You need to be constantly aware of the real meaning of terms, and their use within a particular context.

Presentation

This relates to how you present yourself in the role of researcher, which might influence the attitude and expectations of the people you involve in your project. Student-researchers should present themselves as just that, and give the correct impression that they are doing the research as an academic exercise which does not have the institutional or political backing to cause immediate action. Practitioner researchers, such as teachers, nurses or social workers, have a professional status that lends more authority and possibly power to instigate change. Do not raise false expectations.

The research situation can also be influential. Stopping people in the street and asking a few standardized questions will not raise any expectations about actions, but if you spend a lot of time with a, perhaps lonely, old person delving into his/her personal history, the more intimate situation might give rise to a more personal relationship that could go beyond the simple research context. Even more expectations can be raised if you are working in a context of deprivation or inequality. Will the subjects begin to expect you to do something to improve their situation?

Dealing with participants

You should treat participants with due ethical consideration, in the way you choose them, deal with them personally and how you use the information they provide. In many cases, participants choose freely whether to take part in a survey by simply responding to the form or not.

However, friends or relatives may feel that they have an obligation to help you despite reservations they may have and this could result in a restriction of their freedom to refuse. Pressure might be exerted on participants if they are left too little time for due consideration, which might also result in them regretting taking part. Obviously, you should avoid dishonest means of persuasion, such as posing as an official, making unrealistic and untrue promises, being unduly persistent, and targeting people in vulnerable situations. This could occur almost inadvertently if you are not alert to people's situations and reactions.

Participants will decide whether to take part according to the information they receive about the research. The form that this information takes will depend on the type of person, the nature of the research process and the context. It should be clear and easily understood, so they can make a fair assessment of the project in order to give **informed consent**. Particular attention is needed when getting consent from vulnerable people such as children, the elderly or ill, foreign language speakers and those who are illiterate.

When working within organizations, managers or other people with overall responsibilities may need to be consulted, with the result that several layers of consent will be required. Make it clear and get agreement at all levels about what issues are to be discussed, how the investigation will be conducted, how confidentiality will be maintained. Be aware that there may be conflicts of interest between the management and employees, so there must be some obvious form of protection for those making criticisms of the organization or systems of work or conditions.

Although verbal explanations may be sufficient in informal situations, a written résumé on a flyer could be useful. Questionnaires should always provide the necessary written information as an introduction. Participants must have the right to terminate their participation at any time.

CARRYING OUT THE RESEARCH

Potential harm and gain

The principle behind ethical research is to cause no harm and, if possible, to produce some gain for the participants in the project and the wider field. Therefore, the researcher should assess the potential of the chosen research methods and their outcomes for causing harm or gain.

This involves recognizing what the risks might be; choosing methods that minimize these risks; and avoiding making revelations that could in any way be harmful to the reputation, dignity or privacy of the subjects.

Recording data

There is a danger of simplifying transcripts when writing up data from interviews and open questions. When you clean up and organize the data, you can start to impose your own interpretation, ignoring vocal inflections, repetitions, asides, and subtleties of humour, thereby losing some of the meanings. Further distortion can be introduced by being governed by your own particular assumptions.

Participant involvement

Questions about rapport are raised if your research entails close communication between you, the researcher, and the participants. Will those involved understand the motivation for your actions and do these conform to your own practice? You should not take familiarity so far as to deceive in order to extract information that the participant might later regret giving. Neither should you raise unrealistic expectations in order to ingratiate yourself.

Sensitive material

Information can be thrown up that is of a sensitive nature which, if revealed, could do damage to participants or to other people. Every case will have to be judged individually, but if this information is relevant to the research, it must be presented in such a way that individuals are not damaged by assuring confidentiality and anonymity. In cases of, for example, unfairness, victimization or bullying, it is unwise to get personally involved, but it might be possible to give advice to the participant about who to contact for help, such as a school tutor, trade union or ombudsman.

Honesty, deception and covert methods

Honesty is a basic tenet of ethically sound research, so any type of deception and use of covert methods should be ruled out. Although you might argue that certain information of benefit to society can only be gained by these methods due to obstruction by people or organizations that are not willing to risk being scrutinized, how can you be sure of the benign consequences of the actions? The risks involved make the use of deception and covert methods extremely questionable, and in some cases even dangerous.

Storing and transmitting data

The Data Protection Act (1998) in the UK and equivalent regulations elsewhere cover the conditions regarding collections of personal data in whatever form and at whatever scale. They spell out the rights of the subjects and responsibilities of the compilers and holders of data. The data that you have collected may well contain confidential details about people and/or organizations. It is therefore important to devise a storage system that is safe and only accessible to you. If you need to transmit data, take measures that the method of transmission is secure and not open to unauthorized access.

Checking data and drafts

It is appropriate to pass the drafts of your research report on to colleagues or supervisors for comment, but only with the proviso that the content is kept confidential, particularly as it is not ready for publication and dissemination at this stage. The intellectual independence of the findings of the report could be undermined if you allow sponsors to make comments on a draft and they demand changes to be made to conclusions that are contrary to their interests. It is not practical to let respondents read and edit large amounts of primary data.

Dissemination

Dissemination of your results in the form of conference or journal papers, a website or other types of publication inevitably involves reducing the length of the material, and perhaps changing the style of the writing. You must therefore be careful that the publication remains true to the original and avoid oversimplification, bias towards particular results or even sensationalization.

Disposing of records

A suitable time and method should be decided for disposing of records at the end of the research project. Ideally, the matter will have been agreed upon with the participants as a part of their informed consent, so the decision will have been made much earlier. The basic policy is to ensure that all the data are anonymous and non-attributable. This can be done by removing all labels and titles that could lead to identification. Better still, data should be disposed of in such a way as to be completely indecipherable. This might entail shredding documents, formatting discs and deleting files.

Getting ethics approval

If your research raises ethical issues, then you will have to get ethics approval from your college, university or organization. Each will have their own regulations and methods for gaining approval. The amount of detail that you will need to provide will depend on the level of your studies, the complexity of the research, and the types of participants that you will engage with – whether they are experts you consult or subjects you wish to observe or question. If your research does not involve any participants, then you will not have to go through this process. Normally, there will be a member of staff in your establishment that has responsibility for managing the approval application process, and an ethics committee that makes the decision for approval.

Table 4.2 shows a typical type of application form for ethical approval, which gives you an indication of the amount of information that is required. This level of information is sufficient for a 'light touch' application – research that does not involve vulnerable people, such as children or people with learning difficulties, or patients in medical experiments or procedures. Research projects for dissertations at undergraduate or master's level are unlikely to require this level of detail – you will need to fill in a much shorter form.

You will notice that there is a substantial amount of written material required to accompany the form to describe in detail the precautions you will take to avoid any ethical problems. Obviously, you will need to be quite advanced in your preparation for the fieldwork in your research project to be able to answer these questions and provide the required information.

Table 4.2 Ethics approval application form

	Yes/no
Lay description Provide a brief outline of the project, including what participants will be required to do. This description must be in everyday language which is free from jargon. Please explain any technical terms or discipline-specific phrases. (No more than 350 words):	
Proposed method Please describe your methodology. If it is easier, then do style the method as Stage 1, Stage 2, etc. (No more than 200 words):	
Investigators' research experience and skills List the relevant experience and outline the skills relevant to this project that the researchers and any supporting staff have in carrying out the research and in dealing with any unexpected outcomes that may arise:	
Summary of study findings Please explain how research participants will receive a summary of the study findings when available. This information should be included in the participant information sheet.	
Recruitment: please indicate your recruitment methods	**Yes/no**
Posters or flyers, if yes, **attach a copy**	
Letter of introduction, if yes, **attach a copy**	
Email or social media message, if yes, **attach a copy of the text**	
Other recruitment method? Please give further details:	
Research and other approvals	
Will the research be carried out only at this University?	
If not, where else will it be conducted?	
Has ethical approval been sought elsewhere? If so, please **provide a copy** of that ethical approval	
Do you intend to recruit? – please tick	
A member of a company or organization that needs to give their consent before the research happens? *(If the study includes a school you will need to complete a FULL UREC application – light touch review is not appropriate for your study.)*	
Individuals aged between 16 and 18 who are competent to give their consent	
Students and/or staff at this University over 18	
Other individuals over 18	
If participants are aged over 80 years of age, please explain why this group of participants is being sought:	
Will any parts of the research be provided by independent contractors (e.g. translators or transcribers)? If yes, **please attach details**	

How many participants will be recruited?	
Please provide an explanation for your proposed sample size:	
Please state any exclusion or inclusion criteria:	
Conflicts of interest: please tick –	
Are there any conflicts of interest in your project? *(This would include: staff teaching students on a module, which may cause real or implied conflicts of interest. Reasons of convenience are not considered adequate justification for conducting research in a situation where a dependent relationship exists.)*	
Have you taken any steps in your recruitment method to overcome potential conflicts of interest? If so, **please attach details**	
Are you offering any participants payment or incentives for taking part in the research?	
If yes, please detail what type of incentive and for how much:	
Risk management	
Will you use a questionnaire or survey? If so, **please attach a copy**	
Will you use written or computerized tests? If so, **please attach a copy**	
Will you interview research participants? If so, **please attach a copy of the interview protocol**	
Will you ask any questions of your research subjects that could be harmful or sensitive, e.g. something that might cause a research subject extra stress or upset that they had not anticipated? *(If yes, please attach to this form a draft of your proposed questions, justify the use of potentially stressful issues, and what counselling services you will put in place should your research subjects require them.)*	
Will you audio-record the participant interviews? If yes, **please indicate this on your consent form**	
Will you transcribe their interviews? If yes, **please indicate this on your participant information sheet**	
Will you ask participants for approval of these transcriptions? If yes, **please indicate this on your participant information sheet**	
Will you photograph or video-record participants? If yes, **please indicate this on your consent form**	
Will you ensure that your research method does **not** diminish self-esteem or cause stress to research participants?	
Does this research involve working overseas? If so, please **attach brief details**	

(*Continued*)

Risk assessment	
Have you completed a risk assessment form at Faculty/ Directorate level?	
Are the risks in the research any greater than normal day-to-day interactions?	
If yes, **please detail**:	
Will the Associate Dean for R & KE in your Faculty, or Director monitor your research progress on an annual basis? This is a University requirement.	
Do you intend to interview, where applicable, participants in their place of work?	
If not, **please detail** where interviews will take place:	
Do you intend to interview participants at home? *(If so please attach a brief summary of the health and safety protocol you will use, such as use of mobile phones, staying in contact with a third party, etc.)*	
Informed consent	
Opt-in consent is the University's preferred approach. Opt-out is problematic where no response is assumed as opt-out, as this approach does not reflect a conscious decision by those invited to accept or decline an invitation to participate in research. Requests for opt-out consent will only considered in exceptional cases and a full explanation should be provided.	
Have you attached a copy of the informed consent form?	
Do you intend to seek consent from participants in writing?	
If not, please detail how consent will be sought:	
Confidentiality and/or anonymity	
Confirm that the research participants will be completely anonymous or will their data be anonymized? *(If not, then please indicate why not on a separate sheet, i.e. elaborate on the use of a focus group or symposium, etc. rather than a confidential face-to-face encounter.)*	
Will the research involve de-identified samples of data?	
Will the research refer to participants by pseudonym?	
Will the research give participants the option to be identified in publications?	
On the PI sheet are participants informed about the legal limits of data confidentiality?	
Will all data and codes and codes be kept securely at this University?	
Will access to computer files be by password, or other appropriate levels of protection, only to those leading the project?	
Are there any special arrangements for data confidentiality that the committee need to be made aware of? If so please provide details. *(This might include the use of web-based discussion methods, like blogs, online surveys, open discussions, password protected, etc. Please provide details so that the committee can consider any data protection implications.)*	

Will the principal investigator be responsible for the security of the data collected?	
Will access be by named researcher only?	
Will access be given to people other than the named researcher? If so, please explain:	
Will the data be stored in accordance with University guidelines and data protection legislation?	
Will the data be kept securely for a period of up to 10 years at this University once the project is finished? (As stated in the Code of Practice for Academic Integrity.)	
Is some part of the research being conducted overseas? If so, please clarify how data will be stored securely during fieldwork, and how it will be transferred for secure storage to this University. This should be indicated on the participant information sheet.	
At the end of the research study, will the data to be stored in a secure online repository? *(This should be explained to participants in the information sheet.)*	
Please confirm that you understand and will comply with data protection legislation.	
Research funding	
Is this research project externally funded	
If yes, who is the funder?	
Does this research project require approval from a funding body before commencing?	
If yes, by when and with whom?	
Have you informed research participants about the source of your funding on the PI sheet?	
Checklist of attachments: **The following paperwork should be included to be approved by UREC**	
Any recruitment advertisements (posters, letters of introduction, email message of the day)	
Participant information sheet(s)	
Consent form(s)	
Evidence of external approval(s) for your research to commence	
Research questionnaire(s)	
Interview schedule(s)	
Research protocol(s)	
Please list any other relevant documentation to be included:	

WHERE TO FIND OUT MORE

Although ethical behaviour should underlie all academic work, it is in the social sciences (as well as medicine, etc.) that the difficult issues arise. Researching people and society raises many ethical questions that are discussed in the books below. The first set of books is aimed generally at student and professional researchers, the second set contains examples of more specialized books – though the issues remain much the same for whoever is doing research involving human participants.

Oliver, P. (2010) *The Student's Guide to Research Ethics* (second edition). Maidenhead: Open University Press.
This is an excellent review of the subject, going into detail on all aspects of ethics in research, and providing useful examples of situations where ethical questions are raised. It demonstrates that there are not always simple answers to these questions, but suggests precautions that can be taken to avoid transgressions.

Hammersley, M. and Traianou, A. (2012) *Ethics in Qualitative Research: Controversies and Contexts*. London: Sage.
This explores conflicting philosophical assumptions, the diverse social contexts in which ethical problems arise, and the complexities of handling them in practice. A practical guide to good practice.

Laine, M. de. (2000) *Fieldwork, Participation and Practice: Ethics and Dilemmas in Qualitative Research*. London: Sage.
The main purposes of this book are to promote an understanding of the harmful possibilities of fieldwork; and to provide ways of dealing with ethical problems and dilemmas. Examples of actual fieldwork are provided that address ethical problems and dilemmas, and show ways of dealing with them.

Mauthner, M. (ed.) (2002) *Ethics in Qualitative Research*. London: Sage.
This book explores ethical issues in research from a range of angles, including: access and informed consent, negotiating participation, rapport, the intentions of feminist research, epistemology and data analysis, tensions between being a professional researcher and a 'caring' professional. The book includes practical guidelines to aid ethical decision-making rooted in feminist ethics of care.

Lee-Treweek, G. and Linkogle, S. (eds) (2000) *Danger in the Field: Ethics and Risk in Social Research*. London: Routledge.
Read this if you are going into situations that might be ethically hazardous.

5

FINDING AND REVIEWING THE LITERATURE

The most important reason for doing research is to produce new knowledge and understanding, and to disseminate it to make it available to everyone. When planning a research project, it is essential to know what the current state of knowledge is in your chosen subject as it is obviously a waste of time to spend months producing knowledge that is already freely available. Therefore, one of the first steps in planning a research project is to do a literature review: that is, to trawl through all the available information sources to track down the latest knowledge, and to assess it for relevance, quality, controversy and gaps. The last two will indicate where additional research is required – to try to resolve a controversy or to fill a gap. This chapter explains where to find the necessary information and how to analyse and present it so that you can devise a solid basis for your research project.

LOADS OF INFORMATION!

We are in an age of radical information expansion. Whatever your subject, there can be no excuse that you are faced with a lack of information. The problem lies in where to find relevant information of the right quality. Any trawl through the Internet will demonstrate what a lot of rubbish there is on every subject under the sun. Even a visit to the library or a good bookshop can be a daunting experience. Luckily, you can easily learn how to use sophisticated methods of trawling for the information you need. No need to spend hours in dusty archives, no need to buy lots of expensive books, but there is a need to get skilled in search-and-find techniques and in methods of appraisal.

Where you look will depend on the subject you have chosen. Some sources cover most subjects, others are specialized in a narrow range, and will hence provide more detail. Here is a list of places you can search.

Libraries

Your university or college library – this should be your first choice. Here you will find a huge amount of information and information about all the other information sources listed below. There are also specialist libraries, such as subject libraries in university departments, professional libraries in professional institutions, technical libraries in technical (research) establishments. Local libraries sometimes have special collections of local interest. Try to get the latest publications, unless you have special reasons not to, e.g. historical studies. The information in fast-moving subjects, such as management, business, science and technology will rapidly become obsolete, but in the humanities older publications can have lasting value.

It is no longer sufficient just to visit the shelves to see what is there, even if you have consulted the online catalogue first. There will be a wide range of electronic resources and search facilities provided, backed up by training sessions and leaflets in the use of these. Being adept at making searches will save you lots of time and frustration, as well as ensuring that you get hold of all the latest information you need.

Here are some of the facilities you should investigate:

- **library catalogue** – most libraries now have an electronic catalogue accessed through their computer terminals, often accessible online from elsewhere, too, via the intra- and/or Internet;
- **journals and newspapers** – these are often catalogued and stored separately from the books and may be available online. As they appear regularly, they tend to be very up to date;
- **electronic databases** – these are computer-based lists of publications, on CD-ROM or more usually on the university intranet or the Internet. They contain huge numbers of sources, and are usually searched by using keywords. Some provide only

titles, publication details and abstracts, others provide the full text. Citation indexes list the publications in which certain books and articles have been used as a reference;

- **librarians** – there are often Subject Librarians who have specialist knowledge in specific subject areas – they will be able to help you explore more elusive sources. University libraries usually run free training sessions on all aspects of searching for information.

Information services

Government departments such as Standards Institutes, Records Offices, Statistical Offices provide information for the public. Pressure groups and voluntary organizations often produce publications about their work. Research establishments, professional and trade organizations also release details about latest research.

Museums and galleries – national and local

Apart from the exhibits, museums and galleries usually produce a range of printed and electronic information. They may also have many artefacts that are in store and only accessible by arrangement. Private collections of historical records and artefacts might be found.

People

There are experts in every field. Some will be willing to advise you. Try the members of your own university staff at first, many of whom will be involved in research. Your library will contain guides to professionals and experts. In some cases, local knowledge will be needed – search out the relevant local experts (e.g. local historians, social workers, ornithologists, etc.).

Intranets

Your own university or organization's intranet. These often provide lecture and presentation notes as well as other specialist information produced by their staff, e.g. research papers and professorial lectures.

The Internet

The full gamut of the World Wide Web. With thousands of pages being added every day, the World Wide Web (WWW) is the biggest single source of information in the world. However, the content is of extremely variable quality, and the biggest challenge when using it is to track down good-quality material. You can easily waste hours trawling through rubbish in search of the goodies. Careful use of search terms helps to eliminate the trash. Usually, the more precise your search parameters, the more manageable the search results will be. Not all information on the WWW is free.

Published Internet guides can help you to make the best of this resource (try your library for lists devoted to subject areas). Some are specifically aimed at students and list useful search engines, sites and databases. Any Internet guide becomes quickly outdated. Specialized search engines such as Google Scholar will filter out much of the dross by listing only academic and technical papers from proven sources. One useful trick is to log into your university library before doing searches on Google Scholar. This will flag up the links to the full papers that have been subscribed to by your library, which you can then download. (It certainly works this way at my university!)

Evaluating web sources

Anyone can add pages to the World Wide Web, so how can you judge if the information you have found is reliable? Here are seven different tests you can make to judge the quality of the contents:

1   Is it accurate? Does it say what sources the data are based on? Compare the data with other sources. If it diverges greatly, is there some explanation for this?
2   What authority is it based on? Find out who authored the pages, and whether they are recognized experts or are issued by a reputable organization. Check if other publications are cited or if they provide a bibliography of other articles, reports or books. You may need to track down the 'home page' to get to the details. Web addresses that end in 'ac' (meaning academia) are likely to be university or college addresses and therefore point to

some intellectual credibility – no guarantee of quality, but nevertheless a useful indicator.

3   Is it biased? Many pressure groups and commercial organizations use the Web to promote their ideas and products, and present information in a one-sided way. Can you detect a vested interest in the subject on the part of the author? Find out more about the authors – e.g. does the information about animal experiments come from an antivivisection league, a cosmetics company, or an independent research institute?

4   How detailed is the information? Is the information so general that it is of little use, or so detailed and specialized that it is difficult to understand? Investigate whether it is only fragmentary and misses out important issues in the subject, and whether the evidence is backed up by relevant data. There may be useful links to further information, other websites or printed publications.

5   Is it out of date? Pages stay on the Web until they are removed. Some have obviously been forgotten and are hopelessly out of date. Try to find a date or when it was updated (perhaps on the View-Page Info option on your web browser). Note that some updates might not update all the contents. Check any links provided to see if they work.

6   Have you cross-checked? Compare the contents with other sources of information such as books, articles, official statistics and other websites. Does the information tally with or contradict these? If the latter, can you see why?

7   Have you tried pre-evaluated 'subject gateways'? The information on these sites has been vetted by experts in the relevant subjects, so it can be relied upon to be of high quality. For examples, try www.eldis.org/ and www.scicentral.com/H-02heal.html.

DOING A LITERATURE REVIEW

The oft-repeated instruction to 'do a literature review' belies some of the complexities of the task, but why should you do one? The review that forms part of research proposal, paper, thesis or dissertation is an important introduction to the research project and underpins the argument about why the project is worth doing. It therefore forms a distinctly recognizable section near the beginning and leads on to the more specific and practical description of the research activities. In the dissertation or thesis, usually, one of the first chapters consists of a critical appraisal of the research literature relevant to the research subject under consideration. This is a more extended version of what is required for a proposal or an essay.

To understand the present 'state of the art', you need to read what other people have written about research in your subject and make some kind of assessment of where your research will fit into that body of work. You need to establish that what you are proposing has not been done in the same way before. To do this, you obviously need to find out what has been researched, and how, within the area that you want to investigate. The 'how' is important, because the way previous research has been conducted will provide a useful source of experience in using relevant research methods for collecting and analysing data.

The review can be used to show where you have gained inspiration to develop your ideas – and this does not just have to be only from academic sources. It should also demonstrate that you have a good understanding of the current conceptual frameworks in your subject, and that you can take a stance in placing your work within these. The literature review tends to reveal a lot about the attitude of the researcher and the seriousness of his/her intentions, as well as the level of organization and clarity of thought achieved.

Below is an extract from a much more extended literature review for a PhD thesis by Alma Clavin. Here, she looks at the literature on an important aspect of her study – the health and well-being benefits of gardening and horticulture.

Gardens, horticulture and allotments for promoting health and well-being

'Horticultural therapy' describes the use of plants by trained professions to reach clinically defined goals (Growth Point, 1999). 'Therapeutic horticulture' describes the process where individuals can develop their well-being using plants and horticulture and can be achieved through active or passive involvement (Lewis, 1996; Frumkin, 2001, 2004; Sempik *et al.*, 2002). These concepts have also been linked to the notion of 'therapeutic landscapes' advanced by geographers (Gesler, 1992; Henwood, 2003). Palka (1999: 30) defines therapeutic landscapes as places that 'promote wellness by facilitating relaxation and restoration and enhancing some combination of physical, mental and spiritual healing'. It is in this context that therapeutic environments (such as gardening and allotments) are used to assist people suffering from physical or mental ill health.

The first study to explore the link between horticulture and mental health in 1955 demonstrated significant increases in improved self-esteem, self-confidence and social interaction amongst people with mental health problems and learning difficulties (O'Reilly and Handforth, 1955). The use of green environments as a form of therapy has a strong tradition in the institutional health care arena for people with poor mental health and vulnerable groups such as the elderly (Parr, 2005; Smyth, 2005). There are a multitude of schemes where gardens, allotments and working in natural environments (woodlands, country parks, etc.) are being used as a form of therapy to treat mental illness.

The reported well-being benefits of garden work amongst vulnerable groups span physical, mental and social well-being effects. These include improved self-esteem and self-confidence, development of work and social skills, improved independence, opportunities for emotional expression and reflection, enhanced spiritual and sensory awareness, useful employment, increased physical activity and exercise, better nutrition from the consumption of healthy food, improved opportunities for social interaction (Sempik *et al.*, 2002; Morris, 2003).

In today's high-stress society, there is increasing recognition that horticultural activity need not be strictly clinically-orientated but can be used in a generalized way to improve the well-being of the individual (Parr, 2005; Sempik *et al.*, 2002). This is seen in the establishment of over 1160 community garden sites in the UK and Ireland (Source: FCFCG). Holland (2004: 285) states that such sites could act as a model for the implementation of social, economic and environmental policies at a local level.

Source: Extract from PhD thesis by Alma Clavin (2010).

Note that for every statement based on previous knowledge she has provided a citation, referring to literature that provides evidence to support it. The list of references at the end of her thesis (list not shown here) provides all the information required to track down the original work.

Doing a literature review means not only tracking down all the relevant information but also taking a critical position on the ideas contained therein. The latter is an important step in determining the quality of research evidence. The process involves an objective critique and evaluation of the strengths and weaknesses of a document, to determine its design quality and merits, and its relevance for your research topic.

You will need to evaluate and consider the relevance of the document to your own dissertation question and study objectives. The literature review will need to be carried out in four major directions, not just narrowly confined to your specific subject area. Here they are, arranged from the general to the particular, with their relative importance depending on the nature of your subject:

1   research theory and philosophy – to establish the intellectual context(s) of research related to your subject;
2   history of developments in your subject – to trace the background to present thinking;
3   latest research and developments in your subject – to inform about the current issues being investigated and the latest thinking and practice, to discuss the conflicting arguments, and to detect a gap in knowledge;
4   research methods – to explore practical techniques that have been used, particularly those that might be relevant to your project.

Here is a checklist of useful points for your review:

- Compile an overview of the literature to illustrate the interplay of ideas and major steps in the development of your subject.
- Introduce the important issues of your research problem through the analysis of the literature.
- Explain the general theoretical background to help the reader understand the attitudes behind the reviewed literature and your own philosophical stance.
- Make links across discipline boundaries when doing an interdisciplinary review, rather than keeping each separate and examining them in turn. You may even suggest some new links that need to be investigated.
- Include some account of how the previous research was done, so that you have a precedent for your own approach to methodology. How many references should you have? This depends on

the subject and extent of the review. As the literature review part of a research proposal should be very short and compact due to limitation of space, you are unlikely to be able to cite more than 15–20 authors; 5–10 might even be sufficient in a narrowly defined field. For a literature review chapter of a dissertation or research project, 20–35 references are more likely. The important thing is to select those that are significant for your work.

ANALYSING THE TEXT

A distinction must be made between a review of the literature as a preliminary to a research project, and the detailed analysis of each piece of literature. The latter is a quality control exercise that helps you to choose the best and most relevant pieces of information to use in the review. The point of the detailed analysis is not just to find fault with the style of writing or ideas, but to present a critique, an analysis, or an examination of them; to give your own personal and professional appraisal of the content and quality of the content in question. A description is not enough.

Critical appraisal requires lots of in-depth reading and is a skill that must be learned and practised, which can initially be quite time-consuming. The main steps can be summarized as:

1   Thoroughly read the original research article and decide if it is relevant to your study. Assess whether the purpose of the research is well defined and ensure that the research methods are made clear. Identify the data collection and analysis methods, the findings and the conclusions, and assess their clarity.
2   Reveal the assumptions upon which the writings and arguments are based. All writing is rooted in theory and based on values. Sometimes these are quite clearly stated at the beginning of the text, sometimes they are obscured or not mentioned. Some knowledge of the different theoretical positions is required in order to be able to detect them and know what they imply, e.g. a feminist approach in social science, a Keynesian approach in economics, a modernist approach in architecture and a Freudian approach in psychology.
3   Trace the logic of the argument to ascertain whether the steps in the argument lead from the evidence to the conclusions. You can

do this by first detecting the conclusion indicators (e.g. therefore, it follows that, etc.) to pinpoint the conclusion(s). The main conclusions should normally appear towards the end of the work, though there may be intermediate conclusions scattered throughout. You can then investigate what evidence is given to support the conclusions and whether the evidence is credible, i.e. does it come from reliable sources?

4   Compare it with other work. As there are no absolute values to which you can appeal to make assessments and no clear rules about what is right and wrong, make comparisons between texts in order to highlight the different approaches, levels of thoroughness, contradictions, strength of arguments, implications of theoretical stances and accepted values and types of conclusions.

Presenting your analysis

A review of the literature should introduce the latest concepts and advances in thinking in the chosen subject by citing relevant papers, publications and authors to underpin the description. However, a thorough critical appraisal of the papers investigated will require a more systematic approach. You will need to make a summary that briefly covers your critical appraisal and assessment of the quality of each research paper. It is a good idea to standardize the form of your appraisals using standard headings, such as:

- Study design and assumptions
- Methods of data collection
- Analytical methods
- Main findings
- Conclusions
- The study's strengths and limitations:

    ○   Clarity
    ○   Logic
    ○   Scope

Using this list of headings you can produce a table with the summaries of your critical appraisal of each of the studies so that you can scan across the set of papers. This will then provide a clear and simple framework for making a comparative assessment of the papers. There are several very useful tools and checklists available in the books recommended below, that consist of detailed sets of questions in the form of checklists. Some critical appraisal tools are general, while others focus specifically on appraising particular types of research, such as quantitative research, systematic reviews, qualitative research evidence, etc.

WHERE TO FIND OUT MORE

The following books provide some very useful detail about doing literature reviews. The titles say what they are about.

Ridley, D. (2012) *The Literature Review: A Step-by-Step Guide for Students* (second edition). London: Sage.
Useful strategies are described for efficient reading, conducting searches, organizing information, and writing the review itself. Examples of best and worst practice drawn from real literature reviews are included throughout to demonstrate how the guidance can be put into practice.

Hart, C. (2001) *Doing a Literature Search: A Comprehensive Guide for the Social Sciences*. London: Sage.
A practical and comprehensive guide to writing a literature review which takes the reader through the initial stages of an undergraduate dissertation or postgraduate thesis.

Machi, L. (2009) *The Literature Review: Six Steps to Success*. London: Corwin/Sage.
A compact reference that offers master's- and doctoral-level students in education and the social sciences a roadmap to developing and writing an effective literature review for a research project, thesis or dissertation.

Finke, A. (2014) *Conducting Research Literature Reviews: From the Internet to Paper* (fourth edition). London: Sage.
An accessible but in-depth look at how to synthesize research literature that presents nearly a hundred new online examples and references from the social, behavioural and health sciences.

Dochartaigh, N. (2012) *Internet Research Skills: How to Do Your Literature Search and Find Research Information Online* (third edition). London: Sage.
The open Web is becoming central to student research practice, not least because of its accessibility, and this clear text describes search strategies and outlines the critical skills necessary to deal with such diverse and disorganized materials.

PART II

THE MAIN RESEARCH METHODS

In the following chapters I look specifically at different types of research methods that are commonly used in academic and applied research. You will have gathered from the previous chapters that there are a variety of opinions about what knowledge is and how we can acquire it, so the techniques for collecting data and analysing it are consequently varied.

To start with, in Chapter 6, I look at the raw material of research – data. In order to collect and analyse data, it is important to understand what they are; what their characteristics are; and how they can be measured. I also consider how statements about data can be expressed at different levels of abstraction, from the up-in-the-sky theoretical to the down-to-earth practical.

People have been collecting data on just about everything, and, in this information age, it is easier to access these collections than ever before. So, in Chapter 7, I explain that you do not always need to do the data collection yourself but can rely on that collected by others. Where to find it and how to analyse it are explored, together with how to test it for reliability. But if you do want to collect your own original data, then I describe in Chapter 8 a range of methods for doing so, from asking questions and making observations, to generating your own data through experiments and simulations.

I dedicate Chapters 9 to 11 to the analysis of data. There are distinct differences in how to deal with quantitative and qualitative data, so they have a separate chapter each. Statistics is the science by which quantitative data are most easily analysed, and there are a vast array of tests that can be applied according to the nature of the data and what you want to interrogate it for. In Chapter 9, I briefly explain some of the most common types.

The analysis of qualitative data has not been developed into an exact science, primarily due to the more imprecise nature of this type of data. Different disciplines tend to favour types of analysis that accord best with their concerns and the nature of their data. However, in all cases there is a need to summarize the mass of raw data and display it in a way that can be used to detect patterns or trends. I explain a range of analytical methods that can be applied to qualitative data in Chapter 10.

Using a mixed methods approach raises additional issues, so these are covered in Chapter 11. I explore the different ways that you can use a variety of methods in the same study to answer complex questions for which a single method is not adequate. I include such issues as interdisciplinarity and the blending of methods; how and when such blending is necessary; and what is gained and lost by using this approach.

In Chapters 12 and 13, I discuss the practical issues that you will face when you want to write about your research. Before starting your project, you need to be very clear about what you want to research, why and how. A research proposal is a written account that should make this all clear, not only to yourself, but to your supervisor, client or promoter. I therefore give some useful guidance in Chapter 12 about how to formulate and structure the proposal and how to plan the work to ensure that the project runs smoothly and on time. Chapter 13 is about the written report, paper, dissertation or thesis that marks the end of your research and is an essential part of the research process. After all, what is the point of doing research if no one is told of the outcomes? I explain the art and science of writing up the account of the project, and provide some useful advice on the techniques you can use to make this process easier.

6

THE NATURE OF DATA

We are all aware that we live in an information age. It is said that the amount of information in the world is doubling every month, or is it every week? Who knows? One thing is for sure – we are deluged with the stuff every day. Data is another word for bits of information (singular – datum). Research uses data as the raw material to reach conclusions about an issue. The issue being investigated dictates what data need to be collected.

Although many data appear to be solid fact and permanently represent the truth, this is not the case. Data are not only elusive, but also ephemeral. They may be true for a time in a particular place, as observed by a particular person, but might be quite different the next day. Take, for example, a daily survey of people's voting intentions in a forthcoming general election. The results will differ each day, even if the same people are asked, because some change their minds due to what they have heard or seen in the interim period.

Data are not only ephemeral, but also corruptible. Hearsay, second-hand reports and biased views are often paraded as facts. The further away you get from the event the more likely it is that inconsistencies and inaccuracies creep in. Memory fades, details are lost, recording methods do not allow a full picture to be given, and distortions of interpretations occur.

Because it is dangerous for a researcher to insist that his or her data – and findings derived from them – are infallible, the outcomes of research are often couched in 'soft' statements, such as 'it seems that', 'it is likely that', 'one is led to believe that', etc. This does not mean, however, that the knowledge gained is useless, only that it is not absolutely certain – like most things in life.

LEVELS OF ABSTRACTION

How do data, the raw materials of research, relate to knowledge as a whole? They are part of a hierarchy of information, going from the general to the particular; from abstract to concrete. Understanding this hierarchy makes it possible to break down research problems expressed in theoretical language to more practical components that can be measured in some way. This hierarchy can be expressed as follows:

- **theory** – abstract statements that make claims about the world and how it works. Research problems are usually stated at a theoretical level;
- **concepts** – building blocks of the theory which are usually abstract and cannot be directly measured;
- **indicators** – phenomena which point to the existence of the concepts;
- **variables** – components of the indicators which can be measured;
- **values** – actual units of measurement of the variables. These are data in their most concrete form.

You can see that the briefest statement of a theory will be the most general and abstract, while the detailed components of the statement will become increasingly particular and concrete. Each theory will contain several concepts, each concept several indicators, each indicator several variables, and each variable several values. For example:

- **theory** – poverty leads to poor health;
- **concepts** – poverty, poor health;
- **indicators** of poverty – low income, poor living conditions, restricted diet, etc.;
- **variables** of poor living conditions – levels of overcrowding, provision of sanitary facilities, infestations of vermin, levels of litter, etc.;
- **values** of levels of overcrowding – numbers of people per room, floor area of dwellings, numbers of dwellings per hectare, etc.

Theory

Although the meaning of the term 'theory' is rather imprecise, in research it refers to a statement that makes a claim about a phenomenon. Theories can range from complex, large-scale, well-researched and substantiated claims developed through academic research, to informal guesses or hunches about specific situations. Our understanding of how the world works is based on theories, and much research is concerned with challenging, refining and extending existing theories, or developing new ones.

As theories, statements tend to be expressed in abstract terms. It is necessary to break them down into their constituent parts in order to examine them. Statements are usually made up of concepts and how they relate.

Concepts

A concept is a term for a phenomenon, often quite abstract, such as alienation, socialism, equilibrium, society; but it can also be quite concrete, such as animal, town, income.

We use concepts all the time as they are an essential part of understanding the world and communicating with other people. Many common concepts are shared by everyone in a society, though there are variations in meaning between different cultures and languages. For example, the concept of 'respect' will mean something different to a streetwise rapper than to a noble lord. Some concepts can only be understood by experts in certain disciplines, e.g. dermatoglyphics, milfoil, parachronism, anticipatory socialization, etc.

Concepts should be clearly defined so that they can be understood in the same way by everyone. This is relatively easy in the natural sciences where precise definitions of concepts such as radio waves, acceleration and elements are possible. In the humanities and social sciences, this may be much more difficult – e.g. concepts such as beauty, honour, motivation, kinship, etc. – as their meanings are often based on opinions, emotions, values, traditions and so on.

Indicators

Concepts that are abstract in nature can be difficult to detect, evaluate or measure. Take 'anxiety' as an example. How could you detect this in a person? The answer is to look for indicators – those perceivable phenomena that give an indication that the concept is present. In this example, the signs that might indicate anxiety could be trembling, worried facial expression, pacing up and down, sweating, shortness of breath, etc. In most scientific and technical subjects, indicators are usually well defined and universally accepted. In the humanities and social sciences they often need to be carefully defined in each research project, as this consensus is frequently lacking.

Variables

In order to gauge the extent or degree of an indicator, you will need to find a measurable component. In the case of anxiety, it would be very difficult to measure the level of worry in a person's expression, but you could easily measure their rate of breathing.

In the natural sciences, the identification of variables is usually relatively simple. Area, temperature, speed and velocity are some examples. Some of these may be appropriate to the social sciences, particularly in quantitative studies, e.g. the number of people in a demonstration, type of occupation, income, etc.

Values

The values are the units of measurement used to gauge the variables. The level of precision of a measurement depends on the nature of the variable and the type of values that are appropriate. Certain scientific studies require that variables are measured incredibly accurately, while some social variables might only be gauged on a three-point scale such as 'agree', 'neutral', 'disagree'.

Data, seen as bits of information, can be used at any level of abstraction. Research projects usually start at the more abstract end of the spectrum, move to the more concrete information during the investigation, and return to the abstract in the conclusions. Data that can be manipulated, measured and analysed tend to be more at the values level but, in many subjects in the humanities and social sciences, the variables may be difficult or even impossible to measure with precise values.

You can relate these levels of abstraction to how to structure your research. Your title and main research question will be expressed at a theoretical level, and your sub-questions will be about the separate concepts. To investigate these, you will need to find out what type of measures can be used to assess the existence and scale of the concepts, then the scales that can be used in the measures, i.e. the type

Figure 6.1 Diagram of levels of abstraction

of measurements, and finally the actual measurements that provide the basic data for analysis. Figure 6.1 provides a simple diagram to illustrate the levels of abstraction in your research structure.

PRIMARY AND SECONDARY DATA

Data come in two main forms, depending on their closeness to the event recorded. Data that have been observed, experienced or recorded close to the event are the nearest one can get to the truth, and are called **primary data**. Written sources that interpret or record primary data are called **secondary sources**, which tend to be less reliable. For example, reading about a fire in your own house in the newspaper a day after it occurred will probably give you less accurate information than what you gained by experiencing the event yourself. You will be more informed about the facts and these will not be distorted by someone else's interpretation.

Primary data

We are being bombarded with primary data all day. Sounds, sights, tastes, tactile things are constantly stimulating our senses. We also have instruments to measure what we cannot so accurately judge through our senses, such as clocks, barometers, business accounts, etc.

There are four basic types of primary data, distinguished by the way they are collected:

1   **measurement** – collections of numbers indicating amounts, e.g. voting polls, exam results, car mileages, oven temperatures, etc.;

2   **observation** – records of events, situations or things experienced with your own senses and perhaps with the help of an instrument, e.g. a camera, tape recorder, microscope, etc.;

3   **interrogation** – data gained by asking and probing, e.g. information about people's convictions, likes and dislikes, etc.;

4   **participation** – data gained by the experience of doing things, e.g. the experience of learning to ride a bike tells you different things about balance, dealing with traffic, etc. rather than just observing.

Primary data are the first and most immediate recording of a situation. Without this kind of recorded data, it would be difficult to make sense of anything but the simplest phenomenon or to communicate the facts to others.

Primary data can provide information about virtually any facet of our lives and surroundings. However, collecting primary data is time-consuming and not always possible. Although more data usually mean more reliability, it is costly to organize large surveys and other studies. Furthermore, it is not always possible to get direct access to the subject of research. For example, many historical events have left no direct evidence.

Secondary data

Secondary data are data that have been interpreted and recorded. Just as we are bombarded with primary data, we are cascaded with secondary data in the form of news bulletins, magazines, newspapers, documentaries, advertising, the Internet, etc. These data are wrapped, packed and spun into pithy articles or digestible sound bites. The quality of the data depends on the source and the methods of presentation. Refereed journals containing papers vetted by leading experts and serious journals, such as some professional and trade journals, will have authoritative articles by leading figures. Magazines can contain useful and reliable information or be entirely flippant. The same goes for books – millions of them! They range from the most erudite and deeply researched volumes to ranting polemics and commercial pap. Television and radio programmes vary likewise, as does information on the Internet.

A major aspect of using secondary data is the assessment of the quality of information or opinions provided. This is done by reviewing the quality of evidence that has been presented in the arguments, and the validity of the arguments themselves, as well as the reputation and qualifications of the writer or presenter. It is also good practice to compare data from different sources. This will help to identify bias, inaccuracies and pure imagination. It will also show up different interpretations that have been made of the event or phenomenon.

QUANTITATIVE AND QUALITATIVE DATA AND LEVELS OF MEASUREMENT

Data are also divided into two other categories, referring not to their source but to their characteristics: basically, whether they can be reduced to numbers or presented only in words. This affects the way that they are collected, recorded and analysed.

Numbers are used to record much information about science and society, for example pressures, bending forces, population densities, cost indices, etc. This type of data is called **quantitative data**. Numbers can be analysed using statistical techniques. However, a lot of useful information cannot be reduced to numbers. People's judgements, feelings of comfort, emotions, ideas, beliefs, etc. can only be described in words. These record qualities rather than quantities, hence they are called **qualitative data**. Words cannot be manipulated mathematically, so require quite different analytical techniques.

Quantitative data

Quantitative data can be measured, more or less accurately, because they contain some form of magnitude, usually expressed in numbers. You can use mathematical procedures to analyse the numerical data. These can be extremely simple, such as counts or percentages, or more sophisticated, such as statistical tests or mathematical models.

Although some forms of data are obviously expressed as numbers – e.g. population counts, economic data, scientific measurements, etc. – other forms that seem remote from quantitative measures can also be converted to numbers. For example, people's opinions about the performance of political parties seem to be difficult to quantify. But if a set choice of answers is given in a questionnaire, then you can then count the numbers of the various responses. The data can then be treated as quantitative.

Table 6.1 Set of quantitative data

Name	Test 1 %	Test 2 %	Test 3 %	Average %
Adams, Rolf	35	64	47	49
Boulter, Helen	55	74	63	64
Carter, Jim	45	68	55	56
Durrant, Chris	63	47	64	58
Escaliente, Laura	36	68	37	47
Fuente, Karl	47	57	57	54
Gardiner, Rachel	53	49	70	57

Census figures (population, income, living density, etc.), economic data (share prices, gross national product, tax regimes, etc.), performance data (e.g. sport statistics, medical measurements, engineering calculations, etc.) and all measurements in scientific endeavour are typical examples of quantitative data. Table 6.1 provides a simple example of a set of quantitative data, in this case referring to scores achieved by seven individuals in three tests.

Qualitative data

Qualitative data cannot be accurately measured and counted, and are generally expressed in words rather than numbers. Essentially human activities and attributes such as ideas, customs, mores, beliefs, that are investigated in the study of human beings and their societies and cultures cannot be pinned down and measured in any exact way. These kinds of data are therefore descriptive in character. This does not mean that they are any less valuable than quantitative data; in fact, their richness and subtlety often lead to great insights into human society.

Qualitative research depends on careful definition of the meaning of words, the development of concepts and variables, and the plotting of interrelationships between these. Concepts such as affluence, happiness, comradeship, loyalty, etc., are real and detectable, even if they are difficult to record and measure.

Observation notes, interview transcripts, literary texts, minutes of meetings, historical records, memos and recollections, documentary films, are all typical examples of qualitative data. Some are recorded very close to the events or phenomena, while others may be remote and highly edited interpretations, so assessments of the reliability of these must be made. Also, qualitative data rely on human interpretation and evaluation and cannot be dispassionately measured in a standard way. Checks on the reliability and completeness of qualitative data can be made by consulting a variety of sources of data relating to the same event – this is called triangulation. Table 6.2 illustrates an example of qualitative data, in this case personal reactions to a change of work practices in a factory of various individuals in different roles.

Research, particularly when about human beings, often combines the examination of both qualitative and quantitative data. In fact, there are many types of data that can be seen from both perspectives. For example, a questionnaire exploring people's attitudes to work may provide a rich source of qualitative data about their aspirations and beliefs, but might also provide useful quantitative data about levels of skills and commitment. What is important is that appropriate analytical methods are used for the different types of data you are dealing with.

MEASUREMENT OF DATA

Data can be measured in different ways depending on their type. These are commonly referred to as levels of measurement – **nominal**, **ordinal**, **interval** and **ratio**.

Nominal level

Nominal measurement is very basic – it divides the data into separate categories that can then be compared with each other. By sorting out the data using names or labels, you can build up a classification of types or categories. This enables you to include, or exclude, specific cases in the types and compare them. For example, buildings may be classified into many types, e.g. commercial, industrial, educational, religious, etc. Some definitions allow only two types – called **dichotomous** – e.g. sex (male or female), while others fall into a set number such as marital status (single, married, separated, divorced or widowed). What is important is that every category is distinctive and that there is no overlap between them which makes it difficult to decide where to place a piece of datum. Ideally, it should be possible to categorize all the data, though sometimes you will need a 'remainders' category for those that cannot be so ordered.

Table 6.2 Set of qualitative data

Role	Reaction					
	Ease of work	Speed of work	Duration of work sessions	Level of efficiency	Remuneration
Unskilled factory worker	More complicated work sequence	Takes less time to complete each task	Prefer more tea breaks	Mistakes made because difficult to concentrate for long periods	More difficult to achieve bonus payments
Skilled operative	More logical production stages	Overall reduction in time taken to produce each component	Longer sessions lead to tiredness	Too much time needed preparing and clearing up	Less overtime payments not offset by increase in wages
Supervisor	Easier to control quality	Less time needed in supervision	Less downtime	More productive working	No extra pay for time needed in making changes
Middle management	Fewer consulta-tions required	Greater output per month	More difficult to plan staffing due to long shifts	Fewer wasted resources	Less complicated pay structure
Managing director	Easier to achieve consistent output	Improved overall productivity	Better utilization of staff and machinery	Shorter manufacture times	Greater profit margins

Nominal data can be analysed using simple graphic and statistical techniques. Bar graphs, for example, can be used to compare the sizes of categories and simple statistical properties, such as the percentage relationship of one subgroup to another, or of one subgroup to the total group, can be explored.

Ordinal level

This type of measurement puts the data into order according to a property that they all share, such as size, income, strength, etc. Precise measurement of the property is not required, only the perception of whether one is greater or lesser than the other.

For example, a class of children can be lined up in order of size without measuring their heights; the runners in a marathon can be sorted by the order in which they finished the race. Likewise, we can measure members of the workforce on an ordinal scale by calling them unskilled, semi-skilled or skilled.

The ordinal scale of measurement increases the range of statistical techniques that can be applied to the data.

Interval level

With this form of measurement, the data must be able to be measured precisely on a regular scale of some sort, without there being a meaningful zero. For example, temperature scales: in the Fahrenheit, Celsius and Réaumur scales, the gradation between each degree is equal to all the others, but the zero point has been established arbitrarily. They each precisely measure the temperature, but the nought degrees of each are different. Another example is the calendar date – compare the Chinese and Western calendars.

In the social sciences, some variables, such as attitudes, are frequently measured on a scale like this:

Unfavourable −4 −3 −2 −1 0 +1 +2 +3 +4 Favourable

Despite appearances, you must be cautious to interpret this as a true interval scale, as the numbers are not precise measurements and indicate preferences on an essentially ordinal scale.

The interval level of measurement allows yet more sophisticated statistical analysis to be carried out.

Ratio level

The ratio level of measurement is the most complete level of measurement, having a true zero: the point where the value is truly equal to nought. Most familiar concepts in physical science are both theoretically and operationally conceptualized at a ratio level of quantification, e.g. time, distance, velocity, mass, etc.

A characteristic difference between the ratio scale and all other scales is that the ratio scale can express values in terms of multiples of fractional parts, and the ratios are true ratios. For example, a metre is a multiple (by 100) of a centimetre, a millimetre is a tenth (a fractional part) of a centimetre. The ratios are 1:100 and 1:10. There is no ambiguity in the statements 'twice as far', 'twice as fast' and 'twice as heavy'. Of all levels of measurement, the ratio scale is amenable to the greatest range of statistical tests.

In summary, you can use the following simple test to determine which kind of data measurement you impose on the values of a variable. If you can say that:

- one value is different from another, you have a **nominal scale**;
- one value is bigger, better or more of anything than another, you have an **ordinal scale**;
- one value is so many units (degrees, inches) more, or less, than another, you have an **interval scale**;
- one value is so many times as big, or bright, or tall or heavy as another, you have a **ratio scale**.

Figure 6.2 provides a summary of the levels of measurement.

Units of measurement:

- Nominal: categorize into boxes, names.
- Ordinal: prioritize according to relative values, put into order.
- Interval: sort according to measured value.
- Ratio: measure in relation to a zero value.

Figure 6.2 Levels of measurement

WHERE TO FIND OUT MORE

What counts as data, and what to do with it, is a big subject in research and gets dealt with exhaustively in most books about academic research. Below are some useful other ways of looking at this aspect, without getting too deeply into technicalities.

Seale, C. (ed.) (2012) *Researching Society and Culture* (third edition). London: Sage.

A well explained section on theories, models and hypotheses appears in chapter 5.

Cooper, D.R. and Schindler, P.S. (2013) *Business Research Methods* (twelfth edition). New York: McGraw-Hill.

Chapters 11 and 12 deal in detail with data measurement and scales, with some useful examples given to bring them to life.

Leedy, P.D. and Ormrod, J. (2015) *Practical Research: Planning and Design* (eleventh edition). Harlow: Pearson.

Chapter 4 provides a rather nice philosophical approach to the nature of data.

Blaxter, L., Hughes, C. and Tight, M. (2010) *How to Research* (fourth edition). Buckingham: Open University Press.

The first part of chapter 8 provides another angle on data and its forms.

7

COLLECTING AND ANALYSING SECONDARY DATA
Modern, historical and archival

Secondary data are data that you have not collected yourself. Wherever there exists a body of recorded information (written material or artefacts), there are subjects for study. In fact, historical and archival research depends entirely on secondary data and the interpretation of them. No type of project is done in a vacuum, not even a pure work of art. Therefore, all research studies require secondary data for the background to the study. You will inevitably need to ascertain what the context of your research question/problem is, and get an idea of the current theories and ideas. It is quite common in student-level research to rely on secondary data for the actual research investigations rather than generating new primary data from the field.

One of the advantages of using sets of secondary data in a modern study is that they have been produced by teams of expert researchers, often with large budgets and extensive resources way beyond the means of a single student, so this cuts out the need for time-consuming fieldwork. Data that have been collected over a long period of time will provide the opportunity to do a longitudinal study (tracing the developments over time), which is impossible to do with data collected in short projects. Secondary data can also be used to compare with primary data you may have collected, to triangulate the findings and put your data into a larger context. Data in the public realm are also open to scrutiny by others and are a permanent resource on which to base your research.

The disadvantage is that you miss out on the experiences and skills gained by having to generate your own primary data from real-life situations. The data will also have been collected with a purpose that might not match easily with what you need for your research focus.

Secondary data for historical and archival research provide the raw material for investigating the subject of interest based in the past. There is a common misconception that history is composed of facts, i.e. certain events, dates, personalities, which would mean that historical research is a matter of uncovering these facts from the historical sources. Fortunately, life is much more complicated than that. The sources can only be a guide to the interpretation of past events based on careful analysis and sound argument. Many different interpretations of the same events are possible, depending on the perspective of the researcher, the choice of evidence and the completeness of the data.

Though many sources of data are free, others are costly to acquire and may be difficult to access. When using data from a variety of sources, there are likely to be mismatches in terminology and the way the data have been collected and analysed or interpreted, making aggregation of the data difficult or open to challenge.

As a researcher, you will face several problems when seeking previously recorded modern, historical and archival data. The main of these are:

- **locating and accessing them** – libraries, museums, archives, collections, sites, etc;
- **authenticating the sources** – when, where and by whom they were produced;
- **assessing credibility** – are the sources really what they claim or appear to be, how strong are the indications of originality, what motivation or bias might have influenced them?
- **gauging how representative or significant they are** – what were the original sources and contexts of the events recorded or objects made, in relation to the times?
- **selecting methods to interpret them** – what ways are there to make sense of the data to use as evidence in your argument?

Locating secondary data can be an enormous topic. Activities can involve anything from rummaging through dusty archives in an obscure library, to downloading the latest government statistical data from the Internet or even unearthing city ruins in the desert. Even current data might be difficult to get hold of. For instance, many current economic data are restricted and expensive to buy. To be useful, data sets should have good documentation that includes descriptions of all the variables and codes, as well as the recording methods that were used.

TYPES AND SOURCES OF SECONDARY DATA

There are numerous types of secondary data, the main ones being documentary sources in the form of written and non-written materials, and survey data in the form of statistical information.

*   **written materials** – organizational records such as internal reports, annual reports, production records, personnel data, committee reports and minutes of meetings; communications such as emails, letters, notes; publications, such as books, journals, newspapers, advertising copy, government publications of all kinds, treaties, etc.;
*   **non-written materials** – television programmes, radio programmes, tape recordings, video tapes, films of all types (including documentary, live reporting, interviews, etc.), works of art, historical artefacts, architecture, archaeological sites, etc.;
*   **survey data** – government censuses of population, employment, household surveys, economic data, organizational surveys of markets, sales, economic forecasts, employee attitudes. These may be carried out on a periodic basis, with frequent regularity or continuously, or ad hoc on one-off occasions. They may also be limited to sector, time and area.

It sometimes depends on how you want to use the data whether they should be regarded as primary or secondary data. For example, if you are analysing a work of art in the form of a painting, you could use it as primary data by looking at the subject, materials and techniques used in the painting, the proportions, etc., unique to that specific painting or artist. Alternatively, you could use it as secondary data when examining it for aesthetic trends, as evidence for developments in art history, or as a commentary on the society of the time. The same could be said for pieces of music, films or television programmes.

It is impossible to give a full description of all sources of secondary data, as the detailed nature of the subject of research determines the appropriate source, and, of course, the possible range of subjects is enormous. However, here are some of the principal types of data and the sources where they can be found.

Data sets online

There are several online sites that provide access to data sets from a variety of sources, such as the Data Archive (www.data-archive. ac.uk), which supplies over 4,000 data sets from sources worldwide, including governments, opinion poll organizations, academic researchers, etc. The European Union publishes statistical information on http://ec.europa.eu/eurostat/statistics-explained/index.php/Main_ Page. For international economic and business information, there are sites such as those provided by FT info (http://news.ft.com), Hoovers Online (www.hoovers.com), and Passport, Euromonitor International's gateway to global strategic intelligence (www.portal.euromonitor. com/portal/account/login).

For UK government data sets, see the UK Data Archive (www. data-archive.ac.uk/), which provides details of the results of surveys such as British Social Attitudes, Company Level Industrial Relations, Eurobarometer, the General Household Survey, the International Social Survey Programme, the Labour Force Survey, etc. Within this is a source directed more at social science issues, supplying access to data from major social surveys – CASS (the Centre for Applied Social Surveys – www.natcen.ac.uk/cass). The Office for National Statistics (www.statistics.gov.uk) is also a good source for data, such as the Annual Employment Survey, the UK New Earnings Survey and the Expenditure and Food Survey. The Census Registration Service (www.census.ac.uk) gives details of the national census results held every ten years since 1801. Other countries provide a similar range of their own statistical data, such as France (www.insee.fr) Germany (www.destatis.de) and the USA (https://catalog.data.gov/ dataset/statistical-abstract-of-the-united-states).

There are also numerous organizations that provide survey data ranging from professional bodies such as the Confederation of British Industry (www.cbi.org.uk) and the American Marketing Association (www.marketingpower.com) to international organizations such as the Organization for Economic Cooperation and Development (www.oecd.org) and the United Nations (www.un.org), and advisory and regulating bodies such as the Advisory, Conciliation and

Arbitration Service (www.acas.org.uk) and the Advertising Standards Authority (www.asa.org.uk/).

Don't forget that not all data sets are in the form of lists of statistics. Spatial information is contained on maps and charts. One rich mine of information is the Geographic Information System (GIS), which is a source of much geographical and demographic data for areas throughout the world based on mapping techniques.

Documentary data

Cultural texts

Many of the prevailing theoretical debates (e.g. postmodernism, post-structuralism) are concerned with the subjects of language and cultural interpretation, with the result that these issues have frequently become central to sociological studies. The need has therefore arisen for methodologies that allow analyses of **cultural texts** to be compared, replicated, disproved and generalized. In this context, cultural texts are understood to include any text that reveals cultural meanings. From the late 1950s, language has been analysed from several basic viewpoints: the structural properties of language (notably Chomsky, Sacks, Schegloff), language as an action in its contextual environment (notably Wittgenstein, Austin and Searle) and sociolinguistics and the 'ethnography of speaking' (Hymes, Bernstein, Labov and many others).

It can be argued that historical and archival research has forever been concerned with the meticulous analysis of texts from the past to provide interpretations of culture, lifestyles and events, and it is recognized that these interpretations are products of the times and interests when they were made. For example, nineteenth-century historians mainly stressed national and dynastic events, those of the 1920s–1930s were often more concerned with economic and social aspects, while Marxist historians of the 1960s–1970s stressed the relationships and power struggles between classes. Today, the conditions and day-to-day lives of ordinary people in the past are of great interest.

The meaning of the term 'cultural texts' has been broadened from that of purely literary works to that of the many manifestations of cultural exchange, be they formal such as opera, TV news programmes, cocktail parties, etc. or informal such as how people dress or converse. The main criterion for cultural texts is that one should be able to 'read' some meanings into the phenomena. Texts can therefore include tactile, visual and aural aspects – even smells and tastes. They can be current or historical and may be descriptive or statistical in nature. Any of them can be quantitative or qualitative in nature.

Here are some examples of documentary data that come from a wide range of sources:

- personal documents
- oral histories and traditions
- commentaries
- eyewitness evidence and indirect witness
- diaries
- letters
- autobiographies
- official published documents
- state documents and records
- official statistics
- commercial or organizational documents
- mass media outputs
- newspapers and journals
- maps
- drawings, comics and photographs
- fiction
- non-fiction
- academic output
- journal articles and conference papers
- lecture notes
- critiques
- research reports
- textbooks
- artistic output
- theatrical productions such as plays, opera, musicals
- artistic critiques
- programmes, playbills, notes and other ephemera
- virtual outputs
- web pages
- databases.

Libraries, museums and archives

These are generally equipped with sophisticated catalogue systems that facilitate the tracking down of specific pieces of data or enable a trawl to be made to identify anything which may be relevant. Local libraries often store data and collections of local interest. Museums, galleries and collections often have efficient cataloguing systems that will help your search. Larger museums often have their own research departments that can be of help. Apart from public and academic institutions, much valuable historical material is contained in more obscure and less-organized collections, in remote areas and old houses and specialist organizations. However, problems may be encountered with searching and access in less-organized and private and restricted private collections. The attributes of a detective are often required to track down relevant material, and those of a diplomat to gain access to private or restricted collections.

Some archives are ancient and huge. The Vatican Secret Archives, established during the seventeenth century, have material dating back to the eighth century and boast more than fifty-two miles of shelving! Many national archives were founded more than one hundred years ago and have records going back three or four hundred years. Not all records are easy to read and understand. Many are written in archaic languages, in difficult to read handwriting, or illustrated with enigmatic symbols and diagrams, so you may need to acquire special skills to decipher them. In addition, as they were for specific purposes, it may be necessary to do considerable background research to put them into context (see Figure 7.1).

While there is an ever-increasing effort to digitize historic documents, the huge scale of material means that the most popular, useful or accessible items are prioritized. Older forms of cataloguing persist, such as finding aids – documents put together by archivists with information on the contents of collections, magnetic tape, floppy disks and microfiche. The development of the Internet has made it possible for digitized archives to be made readily accessible from wherever you are. International discussions are being held to establish how best to preserve digitized archives for posterity.

Commercial and professional bodies

These often hold much statistical information, both current and historic. Companies will devise records on many aspects of their business for their own internal use, which might be difficult to access unless you

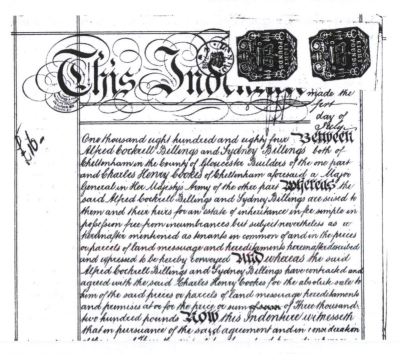

Figure 7.1 The beginning of a property document dated 1844

are a trusted employee. However, trade organizations that represent different branches of industry and commerce usually publish general statistics that refer to the activities of their sector. This is the same with professional bodies, who record many aspects of the professional lives of their members, such as employment trends, levels of commissions and income data.

The data from these bodies are commonly published in report form, both printed and electronic, which can be accessed through their web pages.

SUITABILITY OF DATA FOR YOUR PROJECT

It is worth making several checks before you commit yourself to using secondary data to make sure that the characteristics of the data can fulfil your research objectives and answer your questions:

- **measures** – do the measures match those you need, e.g. economic, demographic, social statistics?

- **dates** – do the data adequately cover the time period being explored?
- **coverage** – are there sufficient data of the required type, and can unwanted data be excluded?
- **population** – is it the same as required for your chosen research?
- **variables** – which are covered? The precise nature of these might not be so important for descriptive work but could be essential for statistical tests or explanatory research.
- **benefits** – will they be greater than your costs?
- **access** – will this be allowed?

AUTHENTICATION AND CREDIBILITY

When you use data from a source where you have had no control in their collection, you will have to assure yourself that they are reliable, sufficiently comprehensive and suitable for your needs. With regard to reliability, a quick assessment can be made by examining the source of the data – what is the reputation of the organization supplying the data? Government statistics and data provided by large, well-known organizations are likely to be authoritative, as their continued existence relies on maintaining credibility. Records held by smaller organizations or commercial companies will be more difficult to check for reliability. In these cases, it is important to make a check on the person or institution responsible for the data, and to explore whether there are any printed publications relating to the research which might give them more credibility.

Although it may be impossible in the case of commercial providers of statistical data, in other cases you should try to undertake an assessment of the methods of collection and analysis used to produce the data. Internet-based data sets may provide this information through hyperlinks, and reports will normally have a section devoted to the research methods used. Issues to be assessed are the sampling method used, the response rate of surveys, the context in which the data were collected and recorded and the analytical methods used to process the data.

The wealth of purely statistical data contained in the archives, especially those of more recent date, provide a powerful resource for research into many issues. You will often find, however, that the recorded data are not exactly in the form that you require (for example, when making international comparisons on housing provision, the data might be compiled in different ways in the different countries under consideration). In order to extract the data you require, you will have to extrapolate from the existing data.

Authentication of historical data can be a complex process, and is usually carried out by experts. A wide range of techniques are used, for example textual analysis, carbon dating, paper analysis, locational checks, cross-referencing and many others.

Credibility of data refers to their freedom from error or bias. Many documents are written to put across a particular message and can be selective of the truth. This may be the case with data acquired from specific interest groups, or reports compiled by those who wish to create a certain impression or achieve particular targets:

> [Documents] should never be taken at face value. In other words, they must be regarded as information that is context specific and as data which must be contextualized with other forms of research. They should, therefore, only be used with caution.
>
> (Forster, 1994: 149)

However, the presence of bias and vested interests in historical texts can be valuable indications of power relationships and ambitions, for example the glorification of a monarch in a contemporary historical account, written to curry favour. Another issue to address in historical data is that today's meanings of words might be different from that of the past, e.g. equality, class, nature, society, etc.

To summarize the process, Figure 7.2 is a diagram with the main questions you should ask when evaluating sources.

When confronted by a document, Lorence (1981) suggests that the student 'should approach the evidence with a skeptical eye, raising such questions as:

1 Who was the witness?
2 To whom (or what audience) was the document addressed?
3 What were the circumstances at the time the document was generated?
4 What was the witness's purpose?
5 Was the witness self-aware? Did he acknowledge his own assumptions?

6 What opportunity did he have to know what he said? What was the witness's position vis-à-vis the subject of his testimony?

7 How much time elapsed between the writing and the actual event?

8 What portion of the evidence is fact, as opposed to conjecture?

9 What probable interest was he defending, if any?

10 Has he acknowledged facts contradictory to his interest or bias?

Much important contextual data can be missing from reports of spoken events, where the pauses, hesitations and gestures are not recorded. The degree of representativeness of the documents should be assessed. This will enable judgements of the generalizability of any conclusions drawn from them to be made.

When using data sets that have been gathered over a period of time, perhaps over years, check that the data collection and analysis methods have remained constant. Any changes in these will alter the resulting data, making comparisons across time more difficult and unreliable. While government and official sources are likely to record

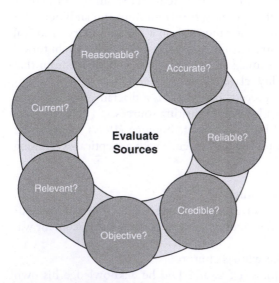

Figure 7.2 Questions to pose when evaluating sources

this kind of change, company and unofficial sources are less likely to do so.

Question whether there is any evidence that the text has been altered or that deletions have occurred, perhaps due to censorship. This can perhaps be revealed when examining how the document relates to other materials from the same era, and whether other contemporary accounts differ. If the document contains references to events or ideas not prevalent when it was alleged to have appeared, these errors will raise questions about the source's reliability.

ANALYSING SECONDARY DATA

Analysis of secondary data can aim to look for patterns or trends across results, to track progression through time, or to seek out the repetition of certain results to build up a strong case. Of the numerous different ways to analyse secondary data, many are no different from those used for primary data, which are described in the later chapters of this volume. However, it is worth mentioning three methods that are particularly suitable for secondary sources: content analysis, data and text mining, and meta-analysis.

Content analysis

Content analysis is a quantitative form of analysis that consists of an examination of what can be counted in text of any form (articles, advertisements, news items, etc.) or other media such as pictures, television or radio programmes or films, and live situations such as interviews, plays and concerts. The analysis is often, but not necessarily, done from secondary sources. The method was developed from the mid-1900s, chiefly in America, and is a rather positivistic attempt to apply order to the subjective domain of cultural meaning. It is done by counting the frequency of phenomena within a case to gauge their importance in comparison with other cases. As a simple example, in a study of racial equality one could compare the frequency of different races in the illustrations in fashion magazines in various European countries. Much importance is given to careful sampling and rigorous categorization and coding in order to achieve a level of objectivity, reliability and generalizability and the development of theories.

There are several basic stages to this method:

- State the research problem, i.e. what is to be counted and why? This will relate to the subject of the study and the relevant contents of the documentary source.
- Employ sampling methods to produce representative findings. This will relate to the choice of publications or other media, the examples selected and the sections within the examples that are investigated.
- Devise the units of analysis. These are the aspects of the content that will be retrieved and recorded in the form of a coding schedule.
- Describe and number the codes that are a measure of the units of analysis in the form of a coding manual.
- Retrieve the coded fragments. This can be done manually, but computer-based search systems are more commonly used when the text can be digitized.
- Do quality checks on interpretation. This covers issues of:

  o the units of analysis (can the selected aspects or themes really be divided from the rest of the text?);
  o classification (are the units counted really all similar enough to be counted together?);
  o combination of data and formation of '100 per cents' (how can the units counted be weighted by length/detail/author-itativeness and how is the totality of the elements to be calculated?).

- Analyse the data (what methods of interpretation will you use?).

Coding schedule, coding manual and tabulation of results

The relevant units of analysis are devised by a preliminary review of the cases, consisting of examples of a type of publication, programme or film. A coding schedule in the form of a table is then set up, with each column being headed by a unit of analysis used to investigate each case. Figure 7.3 is an example of a coding schedule devised for an analysis of the contents of a local television evening news pro-gramme and how the items are reported and illustrated.

Programme date	News item	Duration in mins	Location	Reporting format	On-site reporting	Image	Soundtrack

Figure 7.3 Coding schedule

These units of analysis are then broken down to establish codes that can be used to describe or measure them. A coding manual can then be produced that lists descriptions or measurements in the form of numbered codes that will be searched for and recorded. The codes can consist of a word or a phrase. An example of a possible coding manual derived from the coding schedule in Figure 7.3 is shown in Figure 7.4.

Tabulation of results

The numerical data that form the results of a content analysis are most conveniently presented in tabular form. A separate table is produced for each case based on the coding schedule, with the columns listing the codes filled in (see Figure 7.5). When the results of cases have be tabulated, the frequency of the occurrence of the different codes throughout all the cases can then be counted.

What content analysis on its own cannot do is discover the effects that the publications, programmes, films, etc. have on their audience. Other research methods (e.g. questionnaires, interviews, etc.) must be used to gain this type of information. What it can uncover, however, is how the methods of communication are constructed and which styles and conventions of communication are used by authors to produce particular effects. This form of analysis allows large quantities of data to be analysed in order to make generalizations.

Data and text mining

Data mining is a technique used extensively by business management to extract meaningful information from the huge databases that are generated by electronic and other methods in modern businesses. It is often the starting point in decision-based research. Company data are stored in databases called data warehouses or data marts, containing data from all over the world in international companies.

NEWS ITEM
1 Road accident
2 Burglary
3 Violent crime
4 Civil unrest
5 Drugs incident
6 Terrorist incident
7 Vandalism
8 Political story
9 Health/illness story
10 Job losses
11 Job opportunities
12 Business news
13 Light-hearted story
14 Education story
15 Traffic news
16 Weather news
17 Weather forecast

LOCATION
1 In local region
2 Elsewhere in Britain
3 Abroad

REPORTING FORMAT
1 In studio only
2 In studio introduction to outside reporting

ONSITE REPORTING
1 Journalist report only
2 Witness/victim report(s) only
3 Interview with witness/victim only
4 Expert report only
5 Interview with expert only
6 Mix of journalist report and witness/victim report
7 Mix of journalist report and interview with victim
8 Mix of journalist report and interview with expert

IMAGE
1 Studio only
2 Law court
3 Hospital
4 Ambulance
5 Incident site
6 Home interior
7 Garden
8 Street scene
9 Other location

SOUNDTRACK
1 Only talking
2 Only music
3 Talking and music
4 Added sound effects

Figure 7.4 Coding manual

Programme date	News item	Duration in mins	Location	Reporting format	On-site reporting	Image	Soundtrack
15 Mar	2	3	1	2	6	5	1
	9	2	1	2	4	3	1
	7	2	1	1		1	1
	13	2	1	2	3	7	3
	17	1	1	1		1	1

Figure 7.5 Tabulation of results of a content analysis

Data mining uses statistical tools to explore the data for interesting relationships that can be exploited by the business, such as finding a gap in the market or pinpointing areas of increasing demand. This involves pattern discovery and the prediction of trends and behaviours.

Data visualization techniques help the analyst to gain a clear understanding of the data in pictorial form. These may involve representation of the data in clusters, networks or tree models, or the arrangement of a set of classifications (for example of the characteristics of credit-worthy customers). Underlying patterns in the data may be displayed in the form of associations, often based on market analysis. The patterns might also be considered by taking in the time element and presenting a sequence-based analysis. More complex mining operations employ fuzzy logic, genetic algorithms and fractal-based transformations.

Text mining is used to examine digitized literature and historical written data using computer programs to search for words, phrases or themes in a large volume of texts. There are several techniques that can reveal patterns and usage of words or concepts in different ways to reveal patterns of meaning and contexts in which they are used.

Meta-analysis

Meta-analysis consists of making an analysis of the results of many results of previous research – an analysis of a collection of analyses, hence 'meta'-analysis. This is not the same as a literature review, as it is a statistical analysis of the accumulated data from the results of previous studies rather than a commentary and critical appraisal of the research projects and their outcomes.

The stages in this type of analysis are designed to:

1   define the issue to be investigated – e.g. the effects of class size on student learning;
2   collect the studies according to issue defined at the outset. These may be published or unpublished research results. Care must be taken to select similar studies of good quality, to avoid very different types and qualities of data;
3   find common methods of measurement of variables used to detect significant relationships;

4   select the purpose of analysis of results data, either a comparison to detect how much the results of the studies varied, or to track a particular variable across all the studies and accumulate the results to indicate its importance;

5   carry out the statistical analysis to compare or compute significance levels. An estimation of the size of the effect of one variable on another is a further aspect to be explored. Sometimes it may be useful to divide the studies into sub-groups to clarify the outcomes;

6   report the results and discuss the limitations of the research and recommend further research in the subject.

There are plenty of problems associated with meta-analysis. The main one is that the wide range of methods and statistical techniques used in the various studies make comparison and combination difficult to justify. Another is that the published works only record successful outcomes where statistically significant results are achieved, leaving all the other test results unrecorded. This can lead to an over-optimistic result in the meta-analysis. Despite these, it is a useful way to assimilate the results of numerous studies dedicated to one issue.

Historical method

According to O'Neill, (2015), there are basically three main stages to the method used in historical research:

1   **heuristic** – identifying the relevant material for studying the subject that is the focus of the research. The material can be any historical artefacts that are deemed to be useful in the study, documents, artefacts, sites, etc. The main skill is in the discovery and selection of appropriate material to base the research on;

2   **criticism** – appraising the material in relation to the focus of the study, examining it for authenticity, integrity, bias and context. This appraisal can involve a great deal of background research and investigation into other historic material and previous findings;

3   **synthesis and exposition** – drawing conclusions and communicating the results, using the analysis of the historical material as evidence for the arguments put forward.

It is acknowledged that a definitive account of historic events and conditions cannot be achieved; the aim is to produce the most convincing interpretation of the evidence in the most compact and elegant form. Historical knowledge is in a constant stage of evolution as new finds are made and new, revised or refined explanations are constructed.

WHERE TO FIND OUT MORE

Here are some books that go into more detail about secondary analysis, historical methods and archive research.

Heaton, J. (2004) *Reworking Qualitative Data: The Possibility of Secondary Analysis*. London: Sage.
Provides an emphasis on the reuse of available qualitative data.

Kiecolt, J. and Nathan, L. (1986) *Secondary Analysis of Survey Data* (Sage University Papers). Newbury Park, CA: Sage.
Although a rather old book, this presents useful strategies for locating survey data and provides a comprehensive guide to US social science data archives, describing several major data files. The book also reviews research designs for secondary analysis.

Stewart, D. and Kamins, M. (1993) *Secondary Research Information Sources and Methods* (second edition). Thousand Oaks, CA: Sage.
A comprehensive guide to finding secondary sources, obtaining the sources, and evaluating and integrating the information to answer specific research questions.

What is Secondary Research? (2017). From Data Collection: Low-Cost Secondary Research Tutorial. KnowThis.com. Retrieved 21 January 2017 from http://www.knowthis.com/data-collection-low-cost-secondary-research/what-is-secondary-research
An up-to-date explanation with guidelines particularly aimed at business students.

Faire, L. and Gunn, S. (eds) (2016) *Research Methods for History* (second edition). Edinburgh: Edinburgh University Press.
A comprehensive manual to a wide range of traditional and new digital methods, to help understand how these methods are used and what historical insights they can provide. These methods are also useful for English studies, geography, archaeology and cultural studies.

Ramsey, A., Sharer, W., L'Eplattenier, B. and Mastrangelo, L. (eds) (2010) *Working in the Archives: Practical Research Methods for Rhetoric and Composition*. Carbondale: Southern Illinois University Press.

Although aimed at researchers in rhetoric and composition, this book provides useful general guidance about sourcing, accessing and analysing archives.

Gibbs, F. (n.d.) *A Gentle Introduction to Historical Data Analysis.* Digital poster from George Mason University Fairfax, Virginia. Retrieved 2 February 2017 from http://fredgibbs.net/extras/text-mining-digital-poster.
A simple guide, with examples using computers to do the hard trawling work on texts.

8

COLLECTING PRIMARY DATA

Although we are surrounded by data, in fact, bombarded with them every day from the TV, posters, radio, newspapers, magazines and books, it is not so straightforward to collect the correct data for your purposes. It needs a plan of action that identifies what data you need, where the necessary data are to be found and what are the most effective and appropriate methods of collecting those data. You will need to consider whether to get information from people, in single or large numbers, or whether to observe and/or measure things or phenomena. You may need to do several of these things. For example, in sport you may need to examine not only people, but also their attitudes and fitness and the equipment they use; in commerce, you may be looking at both the product and the production system as well as marketing, sales and distribution – the people and the processes.

There are several basic methods used to collect primary data; here are the main ones:

- asking questions
- conducting interviews
- observing without getting involved
- immersing oneself in a situation
- doing experiments
- manipulating models.

Different disciplines use one or several of these methods to collect data, and customize them to cater for their needs. For example, experiments in social research might be conducted in a natural setting well away from a laboratory, while chemical research might require tightly controlled conditions in order to be successful.

Before we explore the different methods of data collection, we need to consider the issue of selecting who to question or what to examine when faced with a large number of cases.

SAMPLING

If you want to get information about a large group of individual people or things, for example, students or cars, it is normally impossible to get all of them to answer your questions or to examine all the things – it would take much too long and be far too expensive. The solution is to ask or examine some of them and hope that the data you get are **representative** (or typical) of all the rest. If the data you collect really are the same as you would get from the rest, then you can draw conclusions from those answers which you can relate to the whole group. This process of selecting just a small group of cases from out of a large group is called **sampling**.

In other situations, you may want to examine the dynamics within different groups rather than individuals, for instance the social interactions within different neighbourhoods or the processes within different production systems. Here, the individual cases will be groups rather than single people or the things that are members of the group. Again, if you want to draw conclusions about all the cases, you will need to select a few typical ones for detailed study, called **case studies**, using a sampling method. However, in some situations all the cases may be unique, for example different ethnic groups, so it is not possible to find a representative sample. What you can do then is take a comparative approach by selecting several very different cases, e.g. those showing extreme characteristics, those at each end of the spectrum and perhaps one that is somewhere in the middle and compare their characteristics. Alternatively, choose an 'exemplifying' or 'critical' case, one that will provide a good setting for answering the research questions. Results from individual groups might then be compared rather than making generalizations about all the groups. Both quantitative and qualitative methods are appropriate for case study designs, and multiple methods of data collection are often applied.

When doing a survey, the question inevitably arises: how representative is the sample of the whole population? In other words, how similar are characteristics of the small group of cases that are chosen for the survey to those of all the cases in the whole group? When we talk about **population** in research, it does not necessarily

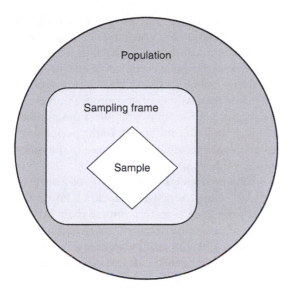

Figure 8.1 Sampling frame in relation to population and sample

mean a number of people; it is a collective term used to describe the total quantity of things (or cases) of the type which are the subject of your study. So, a population can consist of certain types of objects, organizations, people or even events. Within this population, there will probably be only certain groups that will be of interest to your study; for instance, of all school buildings only those in cities, or of all limited companies, only small to medium-sized companies. This selected category is your **sampling frame**. It is from this sampling frame that the sample is selected, as shown in Figure 8.1.

Difficulties are encountered if the characteristics of the population are not known, or if it is not possible to reach sectors of it. Non-representative samples cannot be used to make accurate generalizations about the population. Populations can have the following characteristics:

- **homogeneous** – all cases are similar, e.g. bottles of beer on a production line. It does not matter which cases you select for your sample, as they all have the same characteristics. The larger sample you have, the more chance you will have of finding deviant cases, e.g. in this case it could be bottles not properly filled with beer;

- **stratified** – contain strata or layers, e.g. people with different levels of income: low, medium, high. You can select some cases from each stratum so that you can compare them in some way, e.g. proportion of income spent on accommodation;
- **proportional stratified** – contains strata of known proportions, e.g. percentages of different nationalities of students in a university. To get the right balance in your sample, you select the number of cases in the same proportion as they appear in the population, e.g. to ensure that you get a representative response to questions about the average time students spend exercising;
- **grouped by type** – contains distinctive groups, e.g. of apartment buildings – towers, slabs, villas, tenement blocks. Choose the same number of cases from each type to compare their experiences, e.g. the amount of noise disturbance from neighbours;
- **grouped by location** – different groups according to where they are, e.g. animals in different habitats – desert, equatorial forest, savannah, tundra. Again, choose some cases from each location to compare their habits, e.g. feeding.

With all these types of population, if you know their characteristics, you can choose to select only certain strata or groups for your samples, in the full knowledge that you are leaving out the others, so the data and results of your investigations are only applicable to the chosen ones.

It is generally accepted that conclusions reached from the study of a large sample are more convincing than those from a small one. However, the preference for a large sample must be balanced against the practicalities of the research resources, i.e. cost, time and effort. If the population is very homogeneous, and the study is not very detailed, then a small sample will give a fairly representative view of the whole. If statistical tests are to be used to analyse the data, there are usually minimum sample sizes specified from which any significant results can be obtained. The size of the sample should also be in direct relationship to the number of variables to be studied.

No sample will be exactly representative of a population. If different samples, using identical methods, are taken from the same population, there are bound to be differences in the mean (average) values of each sample owing to the chance selection of different individuals. The measured difference between the mean value of a sample and that of the population is called the **sampling error**, which will lead to bias in the results. **Bias** is the unwanted distortion of the results of a survey due to parts of the population being more strongly represented than others.

There are basically two types of sampling procedure:

1   probability sampling
2   non-probability sampling.

Probability sampling techniques give the most reliable representation of the whole population, while non-probability techniques, relying on the judgement of the researcher or on accident, cannot generally be used to make generalizations about the whole population.

Probability sampling

This is based on using random methods to select the sample. Populations are not always quite as uniform or one-dimensional as, say, a particular type of component in a production run, so simple random selection methods are not always appropriate. The select procedure should aim to guarantee that each element (person, group, class, type, etc.) has an equal chance of being selected and that every possible combination of the elements also has an equal chance of being selected. Therefore, the first question to be asked is about the nature of the population. Is it homogeneous or are there distinctly different classes of cases within it, and, if so, how are they distributed within the population (e.g. are they grouped in different locations, found at different levels in a hierarchy or all mixed up together)? Specific techniques are used for selecting representative samples from populations of the different characteristics, such as simple random sampling, stratified sampling, cluster sampling, etc.

Non-probability sampling

Non-probability sampling is based on selection by non-random means. This can be useful for certain studies, for example, for quick surveys or where it is difficult to get access to the whole population, but it provides only a weak basis for generalization. There are a variety of techniques that can be used, such as **accidental sampling**, **quota sampling** and **snowball technique**.

DATA COLLECTION METHODS

The following sections explore the different methods of primary data collection and briefly describe how they might be applied.

Asking questions – questionnaires

Asking questions is an obvious method of collecting both quantitative and qualitative information from people. Questionnaires are a particularly suitable tool for gaining quantitative data, but they can also be used for qualitative data. This method of data collection is usually called a **survey**. Using a questionnaire enables you to organize the questions and receive replies without having to talk to every respondent. As a method of data collection, the questionnaire is a very flexible tool which has the advantages of having a structured format, being easy and convenient for respondents, and being cheap and quick to administer to a large number of cases covering large geographical areas. There is also no personal influence of the researcher, and embarrassing questions can be asked with a fair chance of getting a true reply. However, questionnaires do require a lot of time and skill to design and develop. They need to be short and simple to follow, so complex question structures are not possible. Not everyone is able to complete questionnaires.

There are three methods of delivering questionnaires, personally, by post or through the Internet. The advantages of personal delivery are that respondents can be helped to overcome difficulties with the questions, and can be persuaded and reminded in order to ensure a high response rate. Obviously, there are problems both in time and geographical location that limit the scope and extent to which this method of delivery can be used. Postal questionnaires are used when many responses are sought, particularly when they are in different locations. The correct address for each respondent is required and postal costs must also be taken into account.

The rate of response for postal questionnaires is difficult to predict or control and they are very prone to low **response rates**, particularly if there is no system of follow-up. It is important that you get a good response rate if you have selected a representative sample. In this case, a poor response rate reduces the reliability of the sample being a true representation of the population. Including a stamped addressed return envelope will help, as will writing a clear and compact covering letter to explain why it is important that the recipient completes and returns the questionnaire and to give assurance about confidentiality. An attractive design, clear instructions for answering questions, and a short length that only requires a few minutes to complete will encourage people to take part. Follow-up reminders normally prompt a number of additional responses.

Internet questionnaires are the cheapest and least time-consuming method of delivery. Although it is easy to get blanket coverage by random delivery, response rates tend to be very low and it is difficult to know how representative the sample will be. For more structured deliveries, email addresses are required to pinpoint responses from the chosen sample. Follow-up reminders are easily administered.

There are basically two question types:

1 **closed format questions** – the respondent must choose from a set of given answers. These tend to be quick to answer, easy to code and require no special writing skills from the respondent. However, they do limit the range of possible answers. The simplest is a bivariate question – with a yes/no answer or just two other kinds of option. Be sure that there are no additional possible options to confuse matters. For a question on gender, male/female used to be all inclusive, but now should you add transgender? When giving any choice of answers, the point remains the same: no categories should be left out, e.g. when asking about party political affiliation, make sure all the political parties are given as options. If this is impossible, add a 'remainders' answer such as 'don't know' or 'other'. You can go further than simple categorization by asking a question that involves ranking.

    example – here are important qualities a prime minister should possess. Number them 1–5 in order of importance – 1 being the most important:

    Honesty, Humour, Intelligence, Consistency, Experience.

    Closed format questions are used to gain quantitative data. Because the answers are predefined, the different responses can be counted and used for statistical analysis;

2 **open format questions** – the respondent is free to answer with their own content and style. These tend to permit freedom

of expression and allow the respondents to qualify their responses. This freedom leads to a lack of bias but the answers are more open to researcher interpretation. They are also more demanding and time-consuming for respondents and more difficult to code.

example – What are the most important qualities a prime minister should possess?

Open questions are used to gain qualitative data. You cannot predict what data the answers will contain, so they will be difficult to accurately categorize and count. Instead they can provide a rich source of data about individual people's opinions, feelings, attitudes, etc.

There are several precautions to take to ensure that the questions can be accurately answered. Avoid asking double questions – impossible to answer both in one answer! Similarly, do not ask questions that are ambiguous by using words that can be interpreted in several ways, e.g. 'your relatives' – to which level of remoteness is intended, or 'dinner' – which can mean a midday meal or evening meal depending on how posh you are! Keep questions short, as no one wants to spend time working out what you mean. Be precise to make sure the respondent knows what you are asking about, e.g. 'What is your standard of living?' will prompt various interpretations of what you mean: level of income, housing conditions, work/home balance, social status, etc. Other types of questions to avoid are leading questions, those including negatives and those using difficult to understand technical terms or acronyms.

It is common practice to pre-test the questionnaire on a small number of people before it is used in earnest. This is called a **pilot study**. Requested feedback from the respondents includes checking for confusion about the reason for the survey, difficulty in understanding the questions, ambiguous wording, complex multiple questions, and inappropriate or incomplete choice of answers. These can then be corrected before the main survey is commenced.

It is important that you get a good response rate, particularly if you have selected a representative sample. In this case, a poor response reduces the reliability of being a true representation of the population. Postal and Internet questionnaire surveys are particularly prone to low response rates, but there are some precautions you can take to maximize returns.

There are many guides that provide standard templates for questionnaires, information on setting them up, how to design them for ease of analysis of the responses, ways to deliver and collect them, and ways to maximize response rates. When I Googled 'questionnaire design', I got over eleven million results! In order to simplify matters for you, I have suggested a few guides at the end of this chapter, some of them aimed at a particular discipline. Online questionnaire programs (such as Survey Monkey, eSurveysPro, SurveyExpression) have free options and are easy to use; they provide templates and basic analysis of the responses as part of their program, saving you much time and effort. You can also export the data as a spreadsheet for further analysis.

Questionnaires are commonly used in disciplines that are concerned with people, particularly as part of society. Research in social sciences, politics, business, healthcare, etc. often needs to gain the opinions, feelings and reactions of a large number of people and this most easily done with a survey. When the government wants to get answers from everyone in the population, then this kind of survey is called a census.

Accounts and diaries

Asking people to relate their account of a situation or getting them to keep diaries is perhaps the most open form of questionnaire. These qualitative data collection methods are used to find information on people's actions and feelings by asking them to give their own interpretation, or account, of what they experience.

Accounts can consist of a variety of data sources: people's spoken explanations, behaviour (such as gestures), personal records of experiences and conversations, letters and personal diaries. If the accounts are authentic, there should be no reason why they cannot be used as an argued explanation of people's actions.

> For example: Trainee nurses are asked to keep a diary of all their activities during a week-long work experience session in a hospital. They are asked to record what they have done in each hour of their working day, and make comments on what they have learned at the end of each day.

Since the information must come directly from the respondents, you must take care to avoid leading questions, excessive guidance and other factors which may cause distortion. You can check the authenticity of the accounts by cross-checking with other people involved in the events, examining the physical records of the events (e.g. papers, documents, etc.) and checking with the respondents during the account gathering process. You will need to transform the collected accounts into working documents that can be coded and analysed.

Diaries are written accounts that usually record events over time. They can take several forms. The most structured form is a response to a series of questions posed by the researcher, prompting the diarist to limit responses to the issues raised by the questions. Both quantitative and qualitative data can be collected this way. Less restricted but still focused in purpose is the log book approach, in which the diarist records the sequence of a specific activity over time, recording tasks undertaken, timing, and possibly reflections about these. The least structured is a diary that is written without any guidance. This is the often the case with personal diaries in the form of historic documents used by historians, but can also be used in social studies as a very open form of gaining contemporary information on attitudes and opinions about life and events.

Conducting interviews

While questionnaire surveys are relatively easy to organize, they do have certain limitations, particularly in the lack of flexibility of response. Interviews are more suitable for questions that require probing to obtain adequate information.

The use of interviews to question samples of people is a very flexible tool with a wide range of applications. Three types of interview are often mentioned:

1   **structured interview** – standardized questions read out by the interviewer according to an interview schedule. Answers may be closed format;
2   **unstructured interview** – a flexible format, usually based on a question guide but where the format remains your choice; you can allow the interview to 'ramble' to get insights into the attitudes of the interviewee. You can probe deeper into interesting aspects, perhaps revealing issues you had not suspected. No closed format questions;
3   **semi-structured interview** – one that contains structured and unstructured sections with standardized and open-type questions.

You can therefore cover standard issues uniformly (such as personal details and basic attitudes) and then expand into more qualitative issues in a flexible way.

Though suitable for quantitative data collection, interviews are particularly useful when qualitative data are required. Interviews can be used for subjects, both general or specific in nature, and even, with the correct preparation, for very sensitive topics. They can be one–off or repeated several times over a period to track developments. As the interviewer and observer, you are in a good position to judge the quality of the responses, to notice if a question has not been properly understood and to encourage the respondent to be full in his/her answers.

Face-to-face interviews can be carried out in a variety of situations: in the home, at work, outdoors, on the move (e.g. while travelling), and they can be used to interview people both singly and in groups. Using visual signs, such as nods, smiles, etc. helps you to get good responses. How you record the responses is a matter of your choice and that of your interviewees. Taking notes can be difficult and is a skill worth practising, as you will be writing at the same time as listening and posing the questions. Making an audio or video recording is easy, but may not be liked by your interviewee. If you rely on your memory, make sure to make notes immediately after the interview, as details are quickly forgotten and you can confuse responses from one interviewee with another.

Focus groups can be seen as a type of group interview, but one that tends to concentrate in depth on a particular theme or topic with an element of interaction. The group is often made up of people who have experience or knowledge about the subject of research, or those that have a particular interest in it, e.g. consumers or customers. You need to be careful to manage the group to allow all the members to provide input.

Telephone interviews avoid the necessity of travelling to the respondents and can therefore be carried out more quickly than face to face. However, you cannot use visual aids to explain questions, and there are no visual clues. For interviewing very busy people, it is best to pre-arrange a suitable time to ring – modern communications technology is making it more and more difficult to talk with an actual person on the phone!

Interviewing by video is now a convenient option that provides a richer experience than contact by telephone. Popular free programs such as Skype, ooVoo, Ekiga, goober, VoxOx, Jitsi and Google Hangouts enable you to see while you talk, and even exchange documents. Group conferences are also possible. Video interviews will take rather more time to arrange than a simple telephone contact, and they are more prone to technical quirks, but they are almost as good as a face-to-face experience, and of course save travelling.

Interviews can be audio recorded in many instances in order to retain a full, uninterpreted record of what was said, but get permission first! However, to analyse the data, you will have to listen to the recording again and possibly transcribe it – a lengthy process if done in full. Recorded and transcribed interviews do not rely on memory and you can repeatedly check what was said. The raw data are also available for different analysis by others.

With every kind of interview, it pays to be well prepared to ensure that you ask all the questions you want to, and to help to keep the interview on track. Figure 8.2 is an example of an interview schedule used by Adi Walker in his PhD study about management of international aid organizations. It is carefully structured on the themes to be covered, and equipped with codes to make storage and retrieval for analysis easy. To save space, I have reduced the width of the notes column, which was big enough for Adi to make his notes straight into the schedule. There were also some opening questions to ensure that the interviewee was well informed about the nature of the study and reason for interview, and assurances about anonymity as outlined in the introductory letter.

Observing without getting involved

This is a method of gathering data through **observation** rather than asking questions. The aim is to take a detached view of the phenomena, and be 'invisible', either in fact or in effect (i.e. by being ignored by people or animals). When studying humans or animals, this detachment assumes an absence of involvement in the group even if the subjects are aware that the observation is taking place. Observation can be used for recording data about events and activities, and the nature or conditions of objects, such as buildings or artefacts. This latter type of observation is often referred to as a survey

Interview code:	Respondent code:	Respondent name:		IHDO:	Date: / /	
Aspect	**Theme**	**Specific/Lead Questions**			**Notes**	**Code**
Intuition	2.1 Intuition for success	2.1.1 Do you agree with the survey findings that intuition is necessary for successful leadership?				IS1
	2.2 Intuition in practice	2.2.1 In which situations or specific contexts do you feel it is acceptable or relevant for leaders to use intuition in decision-making?				IP1
		2.2.2 In which type of circumstances do you think that using intuition is not appropriate or relevant?				IP2
		2.2.3 What do you think are factors that influence your leader to use intuition in his/her work?				IP3
		2.2.4 Can you describe any recent positive and/or negative outcomes from your experiences of your leader using intuition in his/her role?				IP4
	2.3 Developing and measuring intuition	2.3.1 How do you think intuition could be developed in leaders: what specific skills, knowledge, experiences and attributes, and which approaches are required?				ID1
		2.3.2 How do you think intuition could be measured in leader's performance appraisals?				ID2
Versatility	3.1 Versatility for success	3.1.1 Do you agree with the survey findings that versatility is necessary for successful leadership?				VS1
	3.2 Versatility in practice	3.2.1 Which contexts or situations specifically demand that your leader be versatile?				VP2
Characteristics and Competences	4.1 Organisational perspective	4.1.1 Does your organisation have its own set of core leadership characteristics and competences?				CCO1
		4.1.2 If so how is this applied to promote and develop successful leadership?				CCO2
		4.1.3 Does your organisation have and use any kind of bottom up leadership feedback mechanism?				CCO3
		4.1.4 How effective is this in developing the characteristics and competences of your leader(s)?				CCO4
	4.2 Characteristics and competences in practice	4.2.1 The two significantly and unanimously highest rated successful leadership attributes (from 63) were integrity and trustworthiness. Why do you think this is?				CCP1
		4.2.2 Overall, female leaders placed significantly more importance on leadership characteristics for success than their male counterparts, whilst both sexes were quite balanced when it comes to competences. How would you interpret these findings?				OOP2
		4.2.3 Cross, inter and intra-cultural competences are highlighted as factors that affect successful leadership. In which way and to what extent are they promoted and developed in your organisation and/or by your own leader?				CCP3
Influences	5.1 Nurturing key success factors	5.1.1 Leader's action logic (strategic approach to facing challenges) alongside their own competences and characteristics are seen as the main influencing factors on success. How are they nurtured and manifest in your context here?				INS1
	5.2 Cultural dimensions	5.2.1 The culture of the organisation, the leader, the team, and the local context all influence successful leadership. How do these cultural dimensions affect (either positively or negatively) leadership here?				INC1
Locus of leadership	6.1 Definitions	6.1.1 What is your understanding of the differences between leadership roles, functions and tasks?				LD1
	6.2 Perceptions of teams and different organisations	6.2.1 Followers see the leadership role as more successful in the hands of an individual leader, against leaders themselves who see this more as a shared responsibility. What do you think the implications of this are?				LP1
		6.2.2 Humanitarian, transitional (mixed), and development organisations differed significantly in their opinions about where leadership tasks are most successfully handled. Why do you think this is?				LP2
	6.3 Collective vs. individual leadership	6.3.1 What are your opinions about the pros and cons (successfulness) of collective and individual leadership?				LC1
Professionalism	7.1 Definition	7.1.1 What does professionalism signify for you?				PD1
	7.2 Professionalism in practice	7.2.1 Continuous self-development was rated as the highest element of professionalism that contributes to successful leadership. How is this manifest in your own context (organisation, country, your leader)?				PP1
		7.2.2 Humanitarian, transitional (mixed), and development organisations differed significantly in their opinions about the importance of certified entry to the aid sector. Why do you think this is? What are your own opinions?				PP2
	7.3 Professionalism in a future aid sector	7.3.1 Survey respondents stated that professionalism itself needs to be adapted for the sector. What for you should 'aid sector professionalism' look like?				PF1
		7.3.2 How could this 'aid sector professionalism' be applied to result in more successful leadership?				PF2
Wrap up	8.1 Communication protocols	8.1.1 Would you like a transcript of this focus group discussion to approve prior to its further use?				C1
		8.1.2 Would you like a copy of the Doctoral thesis once it is published?				C2
		8.1.3 May I quote you in my research publications? If so, by name, by pseudonym or anonymously?				C3
		8.1.4 If I may quote you, what is your organisations PR protocol for this?				C4
		8.1.5 May I contact you again if I need to clarify something? At which email address?				C5
	8.2 FDG participants Questions	8.2.1 Thank you! And now do you have any questions or other ideas or thoughts you would like to share with me?				Q1

Figure 8.2 Interview schedule

Source: Adi Walker, PhD thesis draft.

(not to be confused with a questionnaire survey), and can range from a preliminary visual survey to a detailed survey using a range of instruments for measurement.

Observation is a basic data collecting activity for many branches of research, particularly the natural and technical sciences; for example, observing the results of experiments, the behaviour of models, the appearance of materials, plants and animals. It is also useful in the social sciences where people and their activities are studied. Using observation, you can record how people react to questions, and whether they act differently from what they say or intend. They can sometimes demonstrate their understanding of a process better by their actions than by verbally explaining their knowledge. Observation can be used to record both quantitative and qualitative data.

Observation is not limited to the visual sense. Any of the senses – e.g. smell, touch, hearing – can be involved, and these need not be restricted to the range perceptible by the human senses. You can use a microscope or telescope to extend the capacity of the eye, just as a moisture meter can increase sensitivity to the feeling of dampness. Instruments have been developed in every discipline to extend the observational limits of the human senses.

> For example: A researcher studying primary education methods records every hour how the space is being used in an infants' open-plan classroom. This is done by describing and sketching the location of the activities on a plan drawing of the room, listing the equipment used and the number of children engaged in each activity.

Observations of objects can be a quick and efficient method of gaining preliminary knowledge or making a preliminary assessment of their state or condition. For example, after an earthquake, a quick visual assessment of the amount and type of damage to buildings can be made before a detailed survey is undertaken. On the other hand, observation can be very time-consuming and difficult when the activity observed is not constant (i.e. you can waste a lot of time waiting for things to happen, or so much happens at once that it is impossible for you to observe it all and record it). Instrumentation can sometimes be devised to overcome the problem of infrequent or spasmodic activity, e.g. automatic cameras and other sensors.

Events and objects are usually complicated, so it is necessary that you identify the variables that are to be studied, and to concentrate on these. It is important that you devise a simple and efficient method of recording the information accurately, particularly when recording frequent or fast-moving events. It may not be possible for you to spend hours and days doing observations, so explore the possibility of observing in periods of time, e.g. one hour in the morning, afternoon and evening, or short periods of time (ten minutes) every hour throughout one day, etc. This is a form of sampling, so it is important to use suitable timing to ensure that you achieve a full impression of the activities. Use instrumentation where and when appropriate; those that make an automatic record of their measurements are to be preferred in many situations.

Immersing yourself in a situation

This is a process of gathering primary data that not only involves observation, but also **experience** in every sense of the word. It is based on the techniques devised by anthropologists to study the social life and cultural practices of communities by immersing themselves in the day-to-day life of their subjects.

Obviously, the observations must be carried out in the natural setting. You try to 'fit in' as much as possible to see and understand the situation from the viewpoints of the group being studied. At its most extreme, the subjects of the study will not be aware that they are being observed by you. Covert methods can be used to disguise your role of observer.

> For example: A researcher wants to find out what the group dynamics are amongst homeless people living on the streets in a large city. He/she poses as a homeless person and joins them in their habitual locations at night, and makes notes on the observations about relationships between the people each day.

In anthropological studies, data are usually collected in phases over an extended period of time. Frequent behaviours, events, etc. tend to be focused on to permit the development of understanding of their significance. Although mostly associated with qualitative approaches, there is no reason why quantitative data are not relevant.

There are a variety of issues that can make the data you collect unreliable or distorted. One commonly mentioned feature is that the behaviour of people might change due to the fact of being knowingly observed. This might not even be a conscious reaction, but could be significant nonetheless. Often it takes time for participants to get used to having an observer around, and they will normalize their behavior after a time. As an observer, you are also exposed to influences that might affect your recording of events. You might have preconceptions that lead you to seek out particular patterns, your memory of events can be inaccurate if you delay recording the data, and you may be influenced by the personalities of those you are observing, e.g. those that are particularly dominant or helpful, or those that are shy and unresponsive. Awareness of these factors will enable you to avoid or minimize them.

Doing experiments

You can collect data about processes by devising experiments. An **experiment** aims to isolate a specific event so that it can be investigated without disturbance from its surroundings. Experiments are primarily aimed at gaining data about causes and effects – to find out what happens if you make a change, why and when it happens, and how.

Experiments are used in many different subject areas, whether these are primarily to do with how things (objects, substances, systems, etc.) interact with each other, or how people interact with things, and even how people interact with other people. Although experiments are commonly associated with work in laboratories where it is easiest to impose control, you can carry them out in almost any other location. It might not even be possible to move the event to be studied into the laboratory, or doing so might unduly influence the outcome of the experiment. For example, some events in nature or social occurrences are so rooted in their context that they cannot be transferred to the laboratory. The design of experiments and models depends very much on the type of event investigated, the sort of variables involved, and the level of accuracy and reliability aimed at practical issues such as time and resources available.

The first step you must take is to identify the essential factors that create the event so that all others can be eliminated or neutralized, something that may be difficult if the context is complicated and you do not know what all the variables are and how they act or are being acted upon. Data are generated when you isolate and manipulate one or more variables that supply the causes (independent variables) and observe the effects of this manipulation on variables that are affected by the causes (dependent variables).

It is important to check that the assumptions you make, on which you base your experiment, are valid. You can do this by introducing a control group, an identical set-up that runs parallel to your experiment, but in which you do not manipulate the independent variables. A common example of this is the use of placebo pills for one group of patients when gauging the effect of a drug on another group. The condition of the patients taking the placebos acts as a 'baseline' against which to measure the effects of the drug on the condition of the other patients.

Internal and external validity

In order to be able to generalize the results beyond the confines of the experiment itself, the experiment should really reflect the situation in the real world – i.e. it should possess both **internal validity** (the extent to which the ideas about cause and effect are supported by the study) and **external validity** (the extent to which findings can be generalized to populations or to other settings).

Internal validity can be undermined by faulty sampling of test materials, the interference of unnoticed factors, deterioration or change in materials during or between tests and faulty instruments. External validity can also be compromised by faulty sampling and unnoticed interfering factors, as well as poor description of the process which makes replicating the experiment impossible, and, when people are the subject of the experiment, changes in the way they act because of the artificiality of the experimental situation.

Laboratory and field experiments

It is not always easy to distinguish between laboratory and field experiments. For example, a social science experiment can take place in realistic simulations of a room in a laboratory, or use a normal setting as a laboratory. There may also be a sense of artificiality in a natural setting when people are organized for the purposes of the experiment, or people are just aware that they are subjects of investigation.

Figure 8.3 Laboratory experiment: testing the airtightness of a cladding system

Laboratory experiments have the advantage of providing a good degree of control over the environment, and of studying the effects on the material or subjects involved. Figure 8.3 shows a laboratory experiment set up to test how much air gets through the joints in a metal cladding system for buildings. Air pressure is raised in the box under the cladding and instruments measure how much pressure is lost due to leakage. This sort of arrangement is ideal when experimenting on inanimate materials, but suffers several possible shortcomings when humans are involved. The experiment can appear to be too artificial and oversimplify the situation, and the experimenter and subjects can introduce bias by their subjective reactions.

In field experiments, subjects are more likely to react and behave normally rather than being affected by artificial conditions. They may also be more willing to take part in the research because they don't need to attend at a particular place and time. External validity is obviously more easily achieved when the experiments are carried out in normal life settings. However, the lack of control and ethical issues can raise some problems. Figure 8.4 shows a hospital waiting area before and after internal planting is added. This was done as part of an experiment to find out if internal planting reduced people's anxiety while they were waiting for a consultation or treatment.

Types of experiments

Experiments are commonly categorized into four types:

1   **True experimental designs** – are characterized by careful random selection of all the cases to be tested, and the use of a control group parallel to the experimental group, which is used to compare outcomes. The groups are also tested before the experiment to determine their properties. All the variables are carefully controlled or neutralized. These are the most reliable designs of experiments, and the data gathered can be relied on to make generalizations.

2   **Quasi-experimental designs** – are used when the random selection of groups cannot be achieved. However, the control group and the experimental group are matched as nearly as possible. If a control group is not used, then parallel groups are

Figure 8.4 Field experiment: testing the effect of indoor planting on waiting patient anxiety (© Jane Stiles)

experimented on to compare the consistency of the outcomes. The results of these designs are not as reliable as true experimental designs.

3 **Pre-experimental designs** – do not have control groups to compare with those that have been experimented on, and some do not even test the experimental group before the experiment. Random selection of the samples may also be omitted. These designs are used when it is not possible to fulfil the conditions of true experimental designs, but the lack of control of the variables can seriously affect the outcomes.

4 ***Ex post facto*** – is not really an experimental approach in that the investigation begins after the event has occurred, so no control

over the event is possible. The search for the cause of the event, e.g. a plane crash or the outbreak of an unknown disease, relies on the search for, and analysis of, relevant data. The most likely cause must be discovered from amongst all possible causes, so there are many opportunities to search in the wrong area!

Manipulating models or simulations

A model, like an experiment, aims to isolate and simplify an event to inspect it in detail and gain useful data. The difference is that models only provide a representation of the event – a simulation – that shows relationships between variables. Models are used to mimic a phenomenon (rather than isolating it as in an experiment) in a form that can be manipulated, to obtain data about the effects of the manipulations. The purpose of a model can be to describe a phenomenon, to serve as a structure for organizing and analysing data, or to explore or test a hypothesis.

As with experiments, it is essential that you understand the system that lies behind the phenomena to be modelled, what the important variables are and how they interact. The actual form of the model can be diagrammatic, physical, or mathematical. Qualitative models emphasize the relationships between entities without trying to quantify them, while quantitative models not only describe the relationships but also accurately measure their magnitude. It is common practice to check the accuracy of the model by comparing the data obtained against data collected from the actual case.

There are three basic types of model:

1   diagramatic models
2   physical models
3   mathematical (or simulation) models.

Diagrammatic models show the interrelationships of the variables in a system on paper. The most familiar type is a technical drawing or a map. Others portray the components of a system and its environment, or show the causal or other links between variables in a system; chart an organization; or even provide a diagrammatic record of a person's thoughts about a particular issue or situation. Diagramming is commonly used to explore a real-life situation in order to investigate

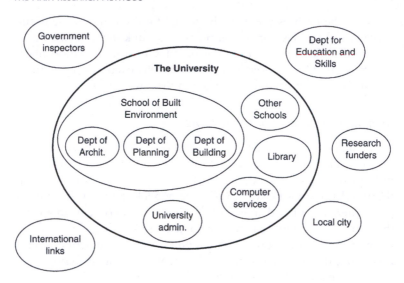

Figure 8.5 Diagrammatic model: systems map of part of a university

what the important variables in the system are and the way in which they influence each other. It promotes the understanding of complicated situations and interrelationships. The understanding gained can often then be used in the construction of a physical or mathematical model. Figure 8.5 is a simple map of the School of the Built Environment within the Oxford Brookes University system.

Physical models are three-dimensional representations of an object at a reduced scale. Models devised for research are specifically designed to test the variables that are central to the problem being investigated. Physical models can be qualitative or quantitative in nature. One of the main problems encountered when designing physical models for producing quantitative data is the problem of scaling. It raises the question, do materials and forms of energy behave identically at any scale? Usually, the answer is no, so the different behaviour of materials at small scale must be compensated for. To overcome the scaling problem, full-scale prototypes are used where possible. Figure 8.6 shows a three-section wooden model of the Festival Hall in London made to scale in order to test the acoustic qualities of the internal space. The sounds, materials and reverberation times all had to be scaled to take account of the smaller size.

Figure 8.6 Physical model: acoustic model of a concert hall (© Kirkegaard Associates)

Mathematical models or **simulations** show the effects of different inputs into a system and predict the resultant outcomes. They are used to predict the weather, the performance of materials under certain conditions, and, combined with physical models, can mimic flying an aeroplane. They are invariably quantitative models and are divided into two major categories: deterministic and stochastic. These categories relate to the predictability of the input – deterministic models deal only with predetermined inputs within a closed system and stochastic models are designed to deal with unpredictable inputs such as the effect of chance or influences from outside the system being modelled. The computer is an invaluable tool for the construction of mathematical models. Spreadsheet programs provide a systematic

Figure 8.7 Computer building simulation output of heat flow through a concrete floor slab

two-dimensional framework for devising models and furnish facilities for cross-calculations, random number generation, the setting of variable values, and the build-up of series of formulae.

Figure 8.7 presents the output from a simulation model that shows the heat flow through a concrete floor slab cooled by buried cold water pipes. You can see by the shaded areas that the slab is coldest around the pipes.

The essential qualities of any model are that it should be constructed for a specific purpose and that it should, in some way, reduce the complexity of the real situation. It is important to clearly explain the purposes of the model, the assumptions on which it is built and the scope of applicability. The same object or event can be modelled in several different ways. Models are never perfect because of the limitations faced by the researcher. These limitations are lack of complete understanding of the variables, inaccuracies of the way their interactions are modelled, and the cumulative effect of small errors in the initial settings of the model.

WHERE TO FIND OUT MORE

This is a big subject and there are innumerable books that deal with every aspect of primary data collection. All the general research methods books will have sections on data collection. Apart from consulting these textbooks, here are some whole books dedicated to different methods.

Finke, A. (2003) *How to Sample in Surveys* (second edition). London: Sage.
This provides a logical progression through the issues raised by sampling techniques and makes good use of examples to illustrate the points made.

Gillham, B. (2008) *Developing a Questionnaire* (Real World Research) (second edition). London: Continuum International.
All you need to know about designing and implementing questionnaires, plus a section on how to relate them to other forms of research.

Azzara, C. (2010) *Questionnaire Design for Business Research: Beyond Linear Thinking – an Interactive Approach*. Oklahoma: Tate Publishing.
This demonstrates how to structure an entire questionnaire, including screening questions, skip logic, test plans, and keeping questionnaires short. In addition, the text walks you through the seventeen answers to the question: 'What's wrong with my questionnaire?'

Oppenheim, A. (2000) *Questionnaire Design, Interviewing and Attitude Measurement* (second edition). New York: Bloomsbury Publishing.
Intended for graduate methodology courses in the social sciences, it is also designed to reach other professionals, including teachers, social workers, medical researchers, and opinion pollsters, who evaluate or carry out social surveys. Its scope also includes interviewing (both clipboard and in-depth interviewing), sampling and research design, data analysis, and a special chapter on pilot work.

Here are some free online survey programs. The trial versions are free, but you can pay for more sophisticated features and freedom from advertising:

Survey Monkey: www.surveymonkey.co.uk
eSurveysPro: www.esurveyspro.com/
SurveyExpression: www.surveyexpression.com/

King, N. and Horrocks, C. (2010) *Interviews in Qualitative Research*. London: Sage.
An accessible and thorough guide to individual and group interviewing, including telephone and online, with examples from social, educational and health sciences. Good section on key debates in the philosophy and theory underlying interview methods.

Orne, J. and Bell, M. (2015) *An Introduction to Qualitative Fieldwork*. Abingdon: Routledge.
Chapters 5, 6 and 7 give good advice about listening, looking and participating.

Simpson, M. and Tuson, J. (2003) *Using Observations in Small-Scale Research: A Beginner's Guide*. Glasgow: Scottish Council for Research in Education.

A short guide on how to transform informal observation into a recognized research tool.

Danny, L. (1989) *Participant Observation: A Methodology for Human Studies*. London: Sage.
Useful manual for if you want to conduct participant observations as part of your research project.

Field, A. and Hole, G. (2003) *How to Design and Report Experiments*. London: Sage.
Clearly explains how to define the research question and choose an appropriate experimental method, design the experiment and analyse the outcomes.

Kirk, R. (2012) *Experimental Design: Procedures for the Behavioral Sciences* (fourth edition). London: Sage.
A comprehensive guide to designing, running and analysing experiments involving people. Suitable for advanced students and practitioners.

Meadows, D. (2008) *Thinking in Systems: A Primer*. London: Chelsea Green.
An introduction to systems thinking and modelling used to understand complex phenomena.

9

QUANTITATIVE DATA ANALYSIS

Quantitative analysis deals with data in the form of numbers and uses mathematical operations to investigate their properties. The levels of measurement used in the collection of the data, i.e. nominal, ordinal, interval and ratio, are an important factor in choosing the type of analysis that is applicable, as is the numbers of cases involved. Statistics is the name given to this type of analysis.

Some of the primary purposes of quantitative analysis are to:

- measure
- make comparisons
- examine relationships
- make forecasts
- test hypotheses
- construct concepts and theories
- explore
- control
- explain.

Most surveys result in quantitative data, e.g. numbers of people who believed this or that, how many children of what age do which sports, levels of family income, etc. However, not all quantitative data originate from surveys. For example, content analysis is a specific method of examining records of all kinds (e.g. documents or publications, radio and TV programmes, films, etc.) that entails counting.

You do not have to be a mathematician to use statistical techniques, as user-friendly computer packages (such as Excel and SPSS – Statistical Package for the Social Sciences) will do all the calculations and presentations for you. However, you must be able to understand the functions of the various tests and displays and their relevance to your own sets of data.

The range of statistical tests is enormous, so only some of the most often used are mentioned here. An important factor to be taken into account when selecting suitable statistical tests is the number of cases for which you have data. Generally, statistical tests are more reliable the greater the number of cases. Usually, more than about twenty cases are required to make any sense of the analysis, though some tests are designed to work with less.

CREATING A DATA SET

In order to manipulate the data, they should be compiled in an easily read form. Although the data will have been organized as part of the collection process, further compilation may be needed before analysis is possible. If the data on the forms cannot be machine read, then it will be necessary to enter the data manually. The fewer steps required in the creation of data sets, the fewer possibilities there are for errors to creep in. Adding codes to response choices on the questionnaire sheet will simplify the transfer of data.

The use of rows and columns on a spreadsheet is the most common technique. A row is given to each record or case and each column is given to a variable, allowing individual cells to contain the data for the case/variable. The data might be in the form of integers (whole numbers), real numbers (numbers with decimal points) or categories (nominal units, e.g. gender, of which 'male' and 'female' are the elements). Missing data also need to be indicated, distinguishing between genuine missing data and a 'don't know' response. It is easy to make mistakes in the rather tedious process of transferring data. It is therefore important to check the accuracy of the data entry. Figure 9.1 shows an example of a simple data spreadsheet with personal details of a range of cases. The numbers are short cuts to the values listed in the key.

PARAMETRIC AND NON-PARAMETRIC STATISTICS

The two major classes of statistics are parametric and non-parametric statistics. You need to understand the meaning of a **parameter** to appreciate the difference between these two types.

Case	Gender	Age	Education	Income
1	1	4	3	4
2	2	5	3	6
3	2	3	4	4
4	2	5	5	3
5	1	6	3	5
6	1	4	2	2
7	1	3	5	4

Key: Gender: Male = 1, Female = 2
Age: 0–18 = 1, 19–25 = 2, 26–35 = 3,
36–45 = 4, 46–55 = 5; 56–65 = 6
66 and above = 7
Education level: None = 1, GCSE = 2
A-level = 3, Degree = 4, Masters = 5
Research degree = 6
Income (annual): 0–5k = 1, +5–10k = 2
+10–20K = 3, +20–40K = 4, +40–60k = 5
Over 60k = 7

Figure 9.1 Data spreadsheet

A parameter of a population (i.e. the things or people you are surveying) is a constant feature that it shares with other populations. The most common one is the **bell** or **Gaussian curve** of normal frequency distribution (see Figure 9.2).

This parameter reveals that most populations display a large number of more-or-less 'average' cases, with extreme cases tailing off at each end. Although the shape of this curve varies from case to case (e.g. flatter or steeper, lopsided to the left or right) this feature is so common amongst populations that statisticians take it as a constant – a basic parameter. Calculations of parametric statistics are based on this feature. Not all data are parametric, i.e. populations sometimes do not behave in the form of a Gaussian curve.

Data measured by nominal and ordinal methods will not be organized in a curve form. Nominal data tend to be in groups (e.g. this is a cow or a sheep or a goat), while ordinal data can be displayed in the form of a set of steps (e.g. the first, second and third positions on a winners' podium). For those cases where this parameter is absent, non–parametric statistics may be applicable (see Figure 9.3).

Figure 9.2 Gaussian curve

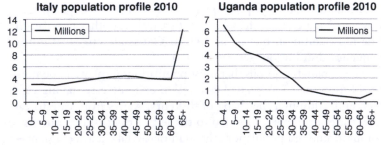

Figure 9.3 Non-parametric data

Non-parametric statistical tests have been devised to recognize the particular characteristics of non-curve data and to take into account these singular characteristics by specialized methods. In general, these types of test are less sensitive and powerful than parametric tests; they need larger samples in order to generate the same level of significance.

STATISTICAL TESTS (PARAMETRIC)

There are two classes of parametric statistical tests: **descriptive** and **inferential**. Descriptive tests will reveal the 'shape' of the data in the sense of how the values of a variable are distributed. Inferential tests will suggest (i.e. infer) results from a sample in relation to a population.

Distinction is also made between the number of variables considered in relation to each other:

- **univariate analysis** – analyses the qualities of one variable at a time. Only descriptive tests can be used in this type of analysis;
- **bivariate analysis** – considers the properties of two variables in relation to each other. Inferences can be drawn from this type of analysis;
- **multivariate analysis** – looks at the relationships between more than two variables. Again, inferences can be drawn from results.

Univariate analysis

A range of properties of one variable can be examined using the following measures.

Frequency distribution

Usually presented as a table, **frequency distribution** simply shows the values for each variable expressed as a number and as a percentage of the total number of cases (see Figure 9.4).

Reason for going regularly to church	Number	per cent
To pray to God	30	28
To be part of a community	25	24
To listen to the sermon	6	6
Because it is a family tradition	9	9
To get away from everyday life	20	19
To take part in and listen to the singing	15	14
Total	105	100

Figure 9.4 Table to illustrate frequency distribution

Measure of central tendency

Central tendency is one number that denotes various 'averages' of the values for a variable. There are several measures that can be used, such as the arithmetic mean (average), the median (the mathematical middle between the highest and lowest value) and the mode (the most frequently occurring value). Normal distribution is when the mean, median and mode are located at the same value. This produces a symmetrical curve (see Figure 9.2). Skewness occurs when the mean is pushed to one side of the median (see Figure 9.5). If there are two modes to each side of the mean and median points, then it is a bimodal distribution. The curve will have two peaks and a valley between.

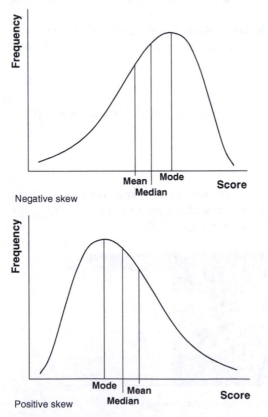

Figure 9.5 Skewness and measures of central tendency

Measures of dispersion (or variability)

The above measures are influenced by the nature of **dispersion** of the values, how values are spread out or bunched up, and the presence of solitary extreme values. Measurements of dispersion can be expressed in several ways: range (the distance between the highest and lowest value); interquartile range (the distance between the top and bottom quarters of the values); and other more mathematical measures such as standard deviation and standard error. These measures do not mean much on their own unless they are compared with some expected measures or those of other variables.

Computer programs provide a choice of display options to illustrate the above measures. The most basic is a summary table of descriptive statistics which gives figures for all the measures. However, more graphical options make comparisons between variables clearer, some of the simpler being:

- **bar graph** – this shows the distribution of nominal and ordinal variables. The categories of the variables are along the horizontal axis (x axis), the values on the vertical axis (y axis). The bars should not touch each other;
- **pie chart** – this shows the values of a variable as a section of the total cases (like slices of a pie). The percentages are also usually given;
- **standard deviation error bar** – this shows the mean value as a point and a bar above and below that indicates the extent of one standard deviation.

Charts and diagrams are far easier to understand quickly by the non-expert than are results presented as numbers (see Figure 9.6).

Bivariate analysis

Bivariate analysis considers the properties of two variables in relation to each other. The relationship between two variables is of common interest in the social sciences, for example: does social status influence academic achievement? Are boys more likely to be delinquents than girls? Does age influence community involvement? There are various methods for investigating the relationships between two variables.

Bar chart

Pie chart

Line chart

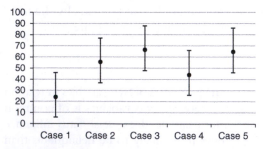

Standard deviation error bar

Figure 9.6 Charts and diagrams

An important aspect is the different measurement of these relationships, such as assessing the direction and degree of association, statistically termed **correlation coefficients**. The commonly used coefficients assume that there is a linear relationship between the two variables, either positive or negative. In reality, this is seldom achieved, but degrees of correlation (i.e. how near to a straight line the relationship is) can be computed. A positive relationship is one where more of one variable is related to more of another, or less of one is related to less of another. For example, more income relates to more political power, or less income relates to less political power. A negative relationship is one where more of one variable is related to less of another or the other way round. For example, more income relates to less anxiety, less income relates to more anxiety. Note that detecting a relationship does not mean you have found an influence or a cause, although it may be that this is the case. Again, graphical displays help to show the analysis.

Scattergrams are a useful type of diagram that graphically show the relationship between two variables by plotting variable data from cases on a two-dimensional matrix. If the resulted plotted points appear in a scattered and random arrangement, then no association is indicated. If, however, they fall into a linear arrangement, a relationship can be assumed, either positive or negative. The closer the points are to a perfect line, the stronger the **association**. A line that is drawn to trace this notional line is called the **line of best fit** or **regression line**. This line can be used to predict one variable value on the basis of the other (see Figure 9.7).

Cross tabulation (contingency tables) is a simple way to display the relationship between variables that have only a few categories. They show the relationships between each category of variables as both number of responses and percentages. In addition, the column and row totals and percentages are shown (see Figure 9.8). As an alternative, the display can be automatically presented as a bar chart.

The choice of appropriate statistical tests that do bivariate analysis depends on the levels of measurement used in the variables. These tests are called by exotic names, e.g. Pearson's correlation coefficient (r), used for examining relationships between interval/ratio variables, and Spearman's rho (ρ), which is used when both variables are ordinal, or when one is ordinal and the other is interval/ratio.

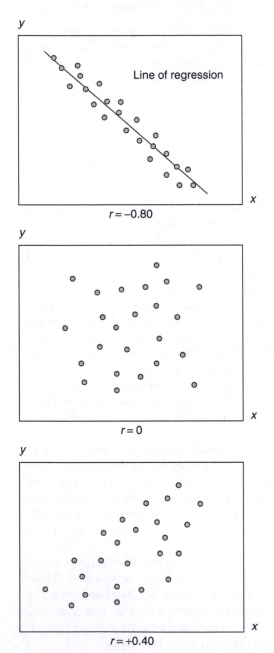

Figure 9.7 Scattergrams of two variables with different levels of relationships

Purchases	Age group			
	Under 25		Over 25	
	No.	%	No.	%
Cosmetics	32	38	2	2
Lingerie	16	19	50	52
Shoes	30	36	32	33
Accessories	6	7	12	13
Total	84		96	

Figure 9.8 Contingency table

Statistical significance

As most analysis is carried out on data from only a sample of the population, the question is raised as to how likely it is that the results indicate the situation for the whole population. Are the results simply occasioned by chance or are they truly representative, i.e. are they **statistically significant**? To estimate the likelihood that the results are relevant to the population as a whole, one has to use statistical inference. The most common statistical tool for this is known as the chi-square test. This test measures the degree of association or linkage between two variables by comparing the differences between the observed values and expected values if no association were present, i.e. those that would be a result of pure chance.

Analysis of variance

The above tests are all designed to look for relationships between variables. Another common requirement is to look for differences between values obtained under two or more different conditions, e.g. a group before and after a training course, or three groups after different training courses. There are a range of tests that can be applied to discern the **variance**, depending on the number of groups.

- For a single group, say the performance of students on a particular course compared with the mean results of all the other courses in the university, you can use the chi-square or the one-group *t*-test.
- For two groups, e.g. comparing the results from the same course at two different universities, you can use the two-group *t*-test, which

compares the means of two groups. There are two types of test, one for paired scores, i.e. where the same persons provided scores under each condition, or for unpaired scores where this is not the case.

• For three or more groups, e.g. the performance of three different age groups in a test, it is necessary to identify the dependent and independent variables that will be tested. A simple test using SPSS is ANOVA (analysis of variance).

The results of the various statistical tests described above are expressed as numbers which indicate the characteristic and strength of the associations.

MULTIVARIATE ANALYSIS

Multivariate analysis looks at the relationships between more than two variables.

Elaboration analysis

This tests the effect of a third variable in the relationship between two variables, for example the effect of gender on the income and level of education of a group of people. This uses a simple tabular comparison by generating two tables and comparing them.

You can continue the process of producing tables for fourth and fifth variables, but this quickly becomes unwieldy and it is difficult to achieve enough data in each table to achieve significant results. There are better ways to understand the interactions between large numbers of variables and the relative strength of their influence using **regression** techniques: multiple regression and logistic regression.

Multiple regression

This is a technique used to measure the effects of two or more independent variables on a single dependent variable measured on interval or ratio scales, e.g. the effect on income due to age, education, ethnicity, area of living, and gender. Thanks to computer programs such as SPSS, the complicated mathematical calculations required for this analysis are done automatically. Note that it is assumed that there are interrelationships between the independent variables as well, and this is taken into account in the calculations. The results can be plotted diagrammatically in a three-dimensional scatterplot, which looks like dots suspended within a cube.

Logistic regression

This method is a development of multiple regression, that has the added advantage of holding certain variables constant in order to assess the independent influence of key variables of interest. It is suitable for assessing the influence of independent variables on dependent variables measured in nominal scale (e.g. whether a candidate's decision to accept a job was determined by a range of considerations such as amount of income, future promotion prospects, level of enjoyment of corporate life, amount of interest in the duties, etc.). The statistic resulting is an odds ratio (e.g. a candidate who was paid more was 3.1 times as likely to accept the job offer than one that was not, assuming all the other variables were held constant).

STATISTICAL TESTS (NON-PARAMETRIC)

Statistical tests built around discovering the means, standard deviations, etc. of the typical characteristics of a Gaussian curve are clearly inappropriate for analysing non-parametric data that do not follow this pattern. Hence, non-parametric data cannot be statistically tested in the above ways.

Non-parametric statistical tests are used when:

- the sample size is very small
- few assumptions can be made about the data
- data are rank ordered or nominal
- samples are taken from several different populations
- there are significant outliers.

For doing these tests, there is an assumption that the data come from an independent random sample, and that when you compare groups, the data for all groups have the same spread (dispersion). The levels of measurement of the variables, the number of samples, whether they are related or independent are all factors which determine which tests are appropriate. This is perhaps a good place to warn you that computer statistical packages (e.g. SPSS) will not distinguish between different types of parametric and non-parametric data. In order to avoid producing reams of impressive looking – though meaningless – analytical output, it is up to you to ensure that the tests are appropriate for the type of data you have.

Some of the tests that you may encounter are: Kolmogorov–Smirnov (used to test a two-sample case with independent samples, the values of which are ordinal), Kruskal–Wallis (an equivalent of the analysis of variance on independent samples, with variables measured on the ordinal scale), Cramer coefficient (gives measures of association of variables with nominal categories) and Spearman and Kendall (which provide a range of tests to measure associations such as rank order correlation coefficient, coefficient of concordance and agreement for variables measured at the ordinal or interval levels).

You should note that these tests have less statistical power than equivalent parametric tests. This means that there is more possibility that you will not correctly reject the null hypothesis when it is false, meaning that you are more likely to miss a correlation between two variables when one exists.

QUANTITATIVE ANALYSIS OF TEXT

Moving away from the analysis of numerical data, there is also a way of analysing text (in its widest meaning covering verbal, written and multimedia communications) in a numerical way. This is called **content analysis**. This method of analysis is particularly useful when you want to compare two or more texts, and it consists of counting how many appearances there are of chosen codes, characteristics, patterns or themes in each. The frequency of the chosen phenomena within each text is noted in order to gauge their importance in comparison with others, often using statistical analysis. It was developed from the mid-1900s, chiefly in America, and is a rather positivistic attempt to apply order to the subjective domain of cultural meaning. As a simple example, in a study of gender roles, one could compare the frequency of the appearance of women in leading roles in business journals in the UK and USA. Content analysis can uncover how the communications are constructed and which styles and conventions of communication are used by authors to produce particular effects. It allows large quantities of data to be analysed to make generalizations.

Careful sampling and rigorous categorization and coding are required to achieve a level of objectivity, reliability and generalizability, and the development of theories. There are a series of basic stages to this method:

1   Ensure that the method is appropriate for what you want to investigate.
2   Choose the appropriate type of material that is to be analysed.
3   Decide on the method of analysis.
4   Select a sampling method and the sample in order to produce representative findings.
5   Decide what is to be counted (units) and why.
6   Work out the system of counting, whether manually, visually or by computer-based searches in the case of digitized text.
7   Do a test run on some data and assess practicality, reliability of interpretation, etc. These quality checks will review the units of analysis (can the units really be divided from the rest of the text?), classification (are the units counted really all similar enough to be counted together?) and combination of data and formation of '100 per cents'. (How can the units counted be weighted by length/detail/authoritativeness and how is the totality of the elements to be calculated?)
8   Analyse the data using the method decided on previously.
9   Present and interpret the findings.

There are two basic approaches to coding, one based on deductive content analysis, where the bases for determining the codes are chosen before coding takes place, and the other based on inductive content analysis, where the codes are gradually developed from and continually revised during the coding process. The latter is used when there is little pre-existing knowledge about the subject and requires an element of exploration to discover the appropriate units.

Coding units at their most simple are words, easily spotted and counted devoid of their context. Counting themes is more problematic, as their meanings are likely to be influenced by the context in which they are found. For example, 'support for religious conventions' in the sentence 'the world would be better off if religious conventions were followed' might be seen as sign of an attitude promoting stability when uttered by the Vatican, while being an ominously dangerous attitude promoting radical change when contained in a missive from Islamic fundamentalists. Other coding features that are sometimes taken into account are notation of space, e.g. size of pictures, amount of space dedicated to articles, headline size; and time, e.g. the duration of television adverts, the amount of background music used in films. As the researcher must make many personal judgements about the selection and value of the contents of the texts, it is a good idea for other researchers to check these against their own judgements to assess inter-rater reliability.

The numerical data that form the results of a content analysis are most conveniently presented in tabular form, usually as output from descriptive statistics using a computer statistical program. The units are shown by number of appearances, together with the percentage of the total. Further analysis can be done if the data are designed to be suitable for multivariate analysis, to check for significant associations and relationships between units.

Crano, Brewer and Lac (2014) conclude that 'the value of content analysis lies in its versatility', adding that it can be applied to most types of communication and a wide range of purposes such as tracking policy changes of authoritarian regimes, or resolving disputes about authorship of specific works.

WHERE TO FIND OUT MORE

For more detailed, though straightforward, introduction to analysing quantitative data, see:

Hoy, W. (2015) *Quantitative Research in Education: A Primer* (second edition). London: Sage.
The goal of this text is to dispel notions that quantitative research is too difficult, too statistical and too theoretical, and generate interest and understanding in using this type of research creatively and effectively.

Diamond, I. and Jeffries, J. (2014) *Beginning Statistics: An Introduction for Social Scientists* (second edition). London: Sage.
This book emphasizes description, examples, graphs and displays rather than statistical formulae. A good guide to understanding the basic ideas of statistics.

Salkind, N. (2016) *Statistics for People Who (Think They) Hate Statistics* (fourth edition). Thousand Oaks, CA: Sage.
If you find yourself uncomfortable with the analysis portion of your work, you will appreciate this book's unhurried pace and thorough, friendly presentation.

Knapp, H. (2017) *Introductory Statistics Using SPSS* (second edition). Thousand Oaks, CA: Sage.

This friendly and practical introduction to statistics shows you how to properly select, process, and interpret statistics without heavy emphasis on theory, formula derivations or abstract mathematical concepts. Online tutorial videos, examples, screenshots, and intuitive illustrations help you to 'get the story' from your data as you learn by doing, completing practice exercises at the end of each chapter using prepared downloadable data sets.

Kerr, A., Hall, H. and Kozub, S. (2002) *Doing Statistics with SPSS*. London: Sage. Apart from simple explanations aimed at undergraduates, this book features 14 SPSS lab sessions which demonstrate how SPSS can be used in the practical research context.

Here are some more. I have ordered these in order of complexity, simplest first. The list could go on for pages with ever-increasing abstruseness. You could also have a browse through what is available on your library shelves to see if there are some simple guides there.

Burdess, N. (2010) *Starting Statistics: A Short, Clear Guide*. London: Sage.

Wright, D.B. (2009) *First (and Second) Steps in Statistics*. London: Sage.

Byrne, D. (2002) *Interpreting Quantitative Data*. London: Sage.

Bryman, A. and Cramer, D. (2011) *Quantitative Data Analysis with SPSS Release 17, 18 and 19: A Guide for Social Scientists*. London: Routledge.

Gibbons, J. (1992) *Nonparametric Statistics: An Introduction* (Quantitative Applications in the Social Sciences). Newbury Park, CA: Sage.

For a good guide on how to interpret official statistics, look at chapter 17 on data archives in the following book:

Seale, C. (ed.) (2011) *Researching Society and Culture* (third edition). London: Sage.

And for a collection of actual studies see:

Levitas, R. (1996) *Interpreting Official Statistics*. London: Routledge.

Content analysis is explained in the following:

Neuendorf, K. (2016) *The Content Analysis Guidebook* (second edition). London: Sage.

This provides an accessible core text for upper-level undergraduates and graduate students across the social sciences. It unravels the complicated aspects of content analysis, using step-by-step instructions and practical advice.

Riff, D., Lacy, S. and Fico, F. (2014) *Analyzing Media Messages: Using Quantitative Content Analysis in Research* (third edition). Abingdon: Routledge.
A primer for learning the technique of systematic, quantitative analysis of communication content. Rich with examples of recent and classic applications, it provides solutions to problems encountered in conducting content analysis, and it is written so that you can readily understand and apply the techniques.

10

QUALITATIVE DATA ANALYSIS

This type of research is based on data expressed mostly in the form of words – descriptions, accounts, opinions, feelings, etc. – rather than in numbers. This type of data is common whenever people are the focus of the study, particularly in social groups or as individuals.

It would be convenient if, when doing a research project, every step of the process was completed before moving on to the next in a nice and tidy fashion. However, this rarely happens, particularly if you are an inexperienced researcher learning as you go or are delving into areas of knowledge that are little explored. You will often need to go back and reconsider previous decisions or adjust and elaborate on work as you gain more understanding and knowledge and acquire more skills. But there are also types of research in which a reciprocal process of data collection and data analysis is an essential part of the project. The information gained from analysis of the preliminary data collection leads to better understanding of the situation and helps to determine what further data collection is required. This process is repeated in order to build up an increasingly sophisticated under-standing of the subject of the study. Figure 10.1 shows how this works. You will see that the first part of the research process is similar in all research, though in qualitative research the definition of the concepts and process of investigation will be more tentative and explorative than in quantitative research. It is in the data collection and analysis where the main difference lies. You will see the reiterative process of data collection, theory development and refinement of the research questions that indicates where more data collection is required. This process continues until satisfactory evidence is collected to support the developed theory, which can then lead to drawing conclusions and finalizing the research.

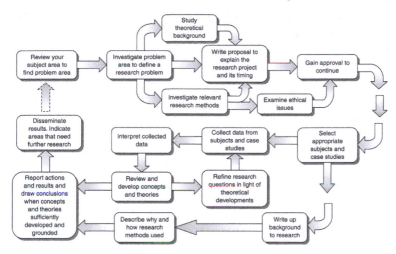

Figure 10.1 Work sequence in qualitative research

If very little is known about the situation, its context and driving forces, and in the absence of previous theories, you can use the **grounded theory** approach, devised in the 1960s (Glaser and Strauss, 1967). Without any preconceptions, you begin with collecting the data from the situation under study and then go on to examine and explain the underlying processes to gain an understanding of what is going on and generate a theory which summarizes this.

Frequently, the situation or process under study is not sufficiently understood initially in order to determine precisely what data you should collect. Therefore, the repeated bursts of data collection and analysis provide you with a greater sensitivity of what is significant and important and allow you to make adjustments to what you need to investigate further, what questions you should ask and what actions to carry out based on what you have already seen, answered and done. This tends to be a demanding and difficult process prone to uncertainties and doubts, and it puts you to the test as much as the data!

Bromley usefully suggests a list of ten steps you should take when carrying out qualitative research (1986: 26):

- Clearly state the research issues or questions.
- Collect background information to help understand the relevant context, concepts and theories.

- Suggest several interpretations or answers to the **research problems or questions** based on this information.
- Use these to direct your search for evidence that might support or contradict these. Change the interpretations or answers if necessary.
- Continue looking for relevant evidence. Eliminate interpretations or answers that are contradicted, leaving, hopefully, one or more that are supported by the evidence.
- 'Cross-examine' the quality and sources of the evidence to ensure accuracy and consistency.
- Carefully check the logic and validity of the arguments leading to your conclusions.
- Select the strongest case in the event of more than one possible conclusion.
- If appropriate, suggest a plan of action in light of this.
- Prepare your report as an account of your research.

As you can see in the list of activities, there are strong links between data collection and theory building. Ideally, the theoretical ideas should develop purely out of the data collected, the theory being developed and refined as data collection proceeds. However, this is difficult to achieve, as without some theoretical standpoint, it is hard to know where to start and what data to collect!

An alternative to this approach is to first devise or select a theory and then test it through the analysis of data collected by field research. In this case, the feedback loops for theory refinement are not present in the process. Even so, theory testing often calls for a refinement of the theory due to better understanding gained by the results of the analysis. There is room for research to be pitched at different points between these extremes in the spectrum.

Although it has been the aim of many researchers to make qualitative analysis as systematic and as 'scientific' as possible, there is still an element of 'art' in dealing with qualitative data. However, in order to convince others of your conclusions, there must be a good argument to support them. A good argument requires high-quality evidence and sound logic. In fact, you will be acting rather like a lawyer presenting a case, using a quasi-judicial approach such as that used in an enquiry into a disaster or scandal.

Qualitative data analysis is required in a wide range of disciplines that deal with people, society and their creations, such as sociology, anthropology, healthcare, the arts, geography, tourism, criminology, marketing, education, theology, philosophy, history and many more.

There are a growing number of computer programs that have been devised for analysing qualitative data. The data are created from all types of qualitative collection methods, whether aural, written or observed; www.predictiveanalyticstoday.com compares their choice of the top twenty-one free qualitative data analysis software packages: QDA Miner Lite, Coding Analysis Toolkit (CAT), Computer Aided Textual Markup and Analysis (CATMA), Aquad, Compendium, Cassandre, LibreQDA, RQDA, TAMS Analyser, ELAN, FreeQDA, Weft QDA, Qiqqa, QCAmap, ConnectedText, Transana, Visão, Tosmana, GATE, Kirq and FsQCA, in no particular order. Different programs are aimed at specific types of qualitative research. They allow codes to be attached to the numbered lines of notes or transcripts of interviews, and for the source of the information/opinion to be noted. This enables a rapid retrieval of selected information from the mass of material collected. They also have linking tools, mapping or networking tools, query tools and writing and annotation tools. Consult your own university IT department for packages and training sessions they provide for students and staff.

STEPS IN ANALYSING THE DATA

How is it possible to organize and analyse qualitative data that is in the form of words, pictures and even sounds, and to come to some conclusions about what they reveal? Unlike the well-established statistical methods of analysing quantitative data, qualitative data analysis is still in its early stages. The certainties of mathematical formulae and determinable levels of probability are difficult to apply to the 'soft' nature of qualitative data, which is inextricably bound up with individual human feelings, attitudes and judgements, and their interplay in society.

Miles and Huberman (1994: 10–12) suggested that there should be three concurrent flows of action:

1   data reduction
2   data display
3   conclusion drawing/verification.

An awkward mass of information that is normally collected to provide the basis for analysis cannot be easily understood when presented as extended text. Information in text is dispersed, sequential rather than concurrent, bulky and difficult to structure. Our minds are not good at processing large amounts of information, preferring to simplify complex information into patterns and easily understood configurations. Therefore, data reduction through coding, clustering and summarizing provides the first step towards simplification, followed by arranging the compacted data into diagrams and tables which can display them in a way that enables you to explore relationships and gauge the relative significances of different factors.

Preliminary analysis during data collection

The process of **data reduction** and analysis should be a sequential and continuous procedure, simple in the beginning stages of the data collection, and becoming more complex as the project progresses. When doing field research, you should keep a critical attitude towards the type and amount of data being collected, and the assumptions and thoughts that brought you to this stage. Raw field notes, often scribbled and full of abbreviations, and tapes of interviews or events, need to be processed in order to make them useful. It is always easier to structure the information while the details are fresh in the mind, to identify gaps and to allow new ideas and hypotheses to develop to challenge your assumptions and biases. Much information will be lost if this task is left for too long.

To begin with, one-page summaries can be made of the results of contacts, e.g. phone conversations, visits. A standardized set of headings will prompt the ordering of the information – contact details, main issues, summary of information acquired, interesting issues raised, new questions resulting from these. Similar one-page forms can be used to summarize the contents of documents.

Typologies and taxonomies

As the data accumulate, the first step is to organize the shapeless mass of information by building **typologies** and **taxonomies**, i.e. classification by types or properties thereby forming subgroups within the general category at a nominal level of measurement. Even the simplest classification can help to organize seemingly shapeless information and to identify differences in, say, types of behaviour or types of people. For example, people in a shopping centre might be classified as 'serious shoppers', 'window-shoppers', 'passers through', 'loiterers', etc. This can help you to organize amorphous material and to identify patterns in the data. Then, noting the differences in terms of behaviour patterns between these categories can help you to generate the kinds of analysis that will form the basis for the development of explanations and conclusions.

This exercise in classification is the start of the development of a **coding** system, which is an important aspect of forming typologies. Codes are labels or tags used to allocate units of meaning to the data, going beyond the simple physical facts. Coding helps you to organize your piles of data; it provides a first step in conceptualization and helps to prevent 'data overload' resulting from mountains of unprocessed data. The process of coding is analytical, and requires you to review, select, interpret and summarize the information without distorting it. There are two essentially different types of coding: one that is used for the retrieval of text sequences, the other devised for theory generation. The former refers to the process of cutting out and pasting sections of text from transcripts or notes under various headings. The latter is a more open coding system used as an index for interpretive ideas – reflective notes or memos, rather than merely bits of text.

The codes you devise will depend on the type of subject and the nature of the study. Often, codes used in similar previous studies can be adopted or adapted. Codes can be used to differentiate between types of acts, activities, meanings, relationships, settings, etc. Normally, a set of codes based on the background study should be devised before doing the fieldwork, and then refined during the data collection process. One important consideration when devising codes is to ensure that they are discrete and unambiguous to make sure that the text fragments or whatever else you are coding can only fit into one code.

Pattern coding

In the next stage of analysis you need to start looking for patterns and themes, as well as explanations of why and how these occur. **Pattern coding** is a method of pulling together the coded information into more compact and meaningful groupings. It reduces the data into smaller analytical units such as themes, causes/explanations, relationships among people and emerging concepts. This allows you to develop a more integrated understanding of the situation and to test your initial answers to the research questions. This helps to provide a focus for later fieldwork and lay the foundations for cross-case analysis in multi-case studies by identifying common themes and processes.

You should find that generating pattern codes is surprisingly easy, as it is the normal way that we process information every day. You can compile notes in the form of **memos**, as a way to explore links between data and to record and develop intuitions and ideas. You can do this at any time – but it is best done when the idea is fresh! Don't cling uncritically to initially developed patterns, but test and develop and if necessary reject them as your understanding of the data develops, and as new waves of data are produced in subsequent data gathering. This 'memoing' should be continued throughout the research project and provide a useful audit trail of the development of your theories.

You will find that the ideas become more stable until you achieve the point where you have reached a satisfactory understanding and explanation of the data, often called the point of saturation. At this juncture, you cannot uncover any further data that can provide additional insights.

Interim summary

At about one-third of the way through the data collection, take stock of the quantity and quality of what you have found out so far, your confidence in the reliability of the data, whether there are any gaps or puzzles left to resolve, and to see what data still need to be collected in relation to your available time. Using this information, produce an **interim summary**, or provisional report, a few pages long, that summarizes for the first time everything you know so far. This is also the first opportunity to make cross-case analyses in multi-case studies and to review emergent explanatory variables. Although the summary will be provisional and probably sketchy and incomplete, it is a useful tool for you to reflect on the work done and to use in discussion with your colleagues and supervisors.

Analysis during and after data collection

Traditional text-based reports are a lengthy and cumbersome way to present, analyse and communicate the findings of a qualitative research project. They present the evidence and arguments sequentially and the information is dispersed over many pages. This presents a problem for both the writer and, especially, the readers, who rarely have time to browse backwards and forwards through masses of text to gain full information. Graphical methods of both data display and analysis can largely overcome these problems by using two-dimensional layouts to order data. They are useful for summarizing, describing, exploring, comparing, as well as explaining and predicting phenomena and can be used equally effectively for one-case and cross-case analysis.

Graphical displays fall into two categories: **matrices** and **networks**.

Matrices (or Tables)

A substantial amount of information can be summarized using two-dimensional arrangements of rows and columns. Matrices can be used to record variables such as time, levels of measurement, roles, clusters, outcomes and effects. They are easy to sketch to any size in a free-hand fashion in order to explore aspects of the data. It is even possible to formulate three-dimensional matrices. You can also use computer programs in the form of databases and spreadsheets to help you in their production and provide neat presentations. For example, Figure 10.2 shows the levels of skills required and amount of help groups got when initiating self-build housing schemes. Six cases are described, and the notes explain the different codes that are used.

Networks

Networks are made up of blocks (nodes) connected by links. These maps and charts can be devised in a wide variety of formats, each with the capability of displaying different aspects of data, such as: processes or procedures, relationships between variables, and causal relationships between important independent and dependent variables. Networks are particularly useful when you compare the results of several case studies, as they permit a certain standardization of presentation, allowing comparisons to be made more easily across the cases.

TASKS: INITIATION AND DESIGN PHASE	grade of difficulty	PET	NVT	GLO	DUN	LTM	DCH
investigation of situation, inception	low	R	P	P	P	P	P
formulation of brief	med	R	P/R	P	P	P/D	P
source land	low	R	P	P	P	P	P
survey site	high	P	P	N	P	P/R	P
design site layout	med	P	P	N	P	D	P
design house plan layout	high	P/R	P/R	P	P	D	P
3D house design	high	P	P	P	P	P	P
construction design	high	P	P	P	P	P	P
structural design	high	P	P	N	P	P	P
planning and building regs applications	high	P	P	P	P	P	P
costing, programming	high	R	P	P	P	P	P
find funds	med	R	P	P	P	P	P
find self-builders	low	R	R	P	P	P	P
select self-builders	med	R	R	P	P	P/R	P
select professionals	low	R	P	P	P	P/R	P

Key skills requirement

R	required skill of self-builders
D	deskilling of task to reduce skill requirement
T	training provided to instill skill
P	professional person allocated to task
N	no requirement for skill and task within the scope of the project

Key skills difficulty grade

LOW	no particular skills, though some instruction necessary
MEDIUM	basic skills requiring limited training and practice
HIGH	sophisticated skills requiring extended training and practice

Figure 10.2 Example of a matrix: self-build skills in six projects

The detail and sophistication of the display can vary depending on its function and on the amount of information available – displays are useful at any stage in the research process. You are free to display the information on networks in the form of text, codes, abbreviated notes, symbols, quotations or any other form that helps to communicate compactly.

Here are some different types of display described by the way that information is ordered within them:

- **Time ordered displays** – record a sequence of events in relation to their chronology. A simple example of this is a project programme giving names, times and locations for tasks of different kinds. The scale and precision of timing can be suited to the subject. Events can be of various types, e.g. tasks, critical events, experiences, stages in a programme, activities, decisions, etc. Figure 10.3 shows a very simple sequence of bringing a product to market.
- **Conceptually ordered displays** – concentrate on variables in the form of abstract concepts related to a theory and the relationships between these. Examples of such variables are motives, attitudes, expertise, barriers, coping strategies, etc. They can be shown as matrices or networks to illustrate taxonomies, content analysis, cognitive structures, relationships of cause and effect or influence, decision trees, etc. Figure 10.4 is an example of a simple influence diagram showing the different types of support provided to disabled people and how they interact.
- **Role ordered displays** – show people's roles and their relationships in formal and informal organizations or groups. A role defines a person's standing and position by assessing their behaviour and expectations within the group or organization. These may be conventionally recognized positions, e.g. judge, mother, machine operator; or more abstract and situation dependent, e.g. motivator, objector. Note that people in different roles tend to see situations from different perspectives. A role ordered matrix will help to systematically display these differences or can be used to investigate whether people in the same or different roles are unified in their views. Figure 10.5 shows the role division in the management of a production company.

- **Partially ordered displays** – are useful in analysing 'messy' situations without trying to impose too much internal order on them. For example, a context chart can be designed to show, in the form of a network, the influences and pressures that bear on an individual from surrounding organizations and persons when making a decision to act. This will help to clarify why a particular action was taken.
- **Case ordered displays** – show the data of cases arranged in some kind of order, according to an important variable in the study. This allows you to compare cases and note their different features according to where they appear in the order.
- **Meta displays** – amalgamate and contrast the data from each case. For example, a case ordered meta-matrix does this by simply arranging case matrices next to each other in the chosen order to enable you to simply compare the data across the meta-matrix. The meta-matrix can initially be quite large if there are a number of cases. A function of the analysis will be to summarize the data in a smaller matrix, giving a summary of the significant issues discovered. Following this, a contrast table can also be devised to display and compare how one or two variables perform in cases as ordered in the meta-matrix.

QUALITATIVE ANALYSIS OF TEXTS, DOCUMENTS, VISUAL MATERIALS AND DISCOURSE

Sources in the form of texts, documents and visual materials provide a great deal of data about society, both historically and in the present. History is preserved in a wealth of archives and documentary evidence, so these methods are particularly important in this field of research. But today, with mass communication and social media,

Figure 10.3 Time ordered display

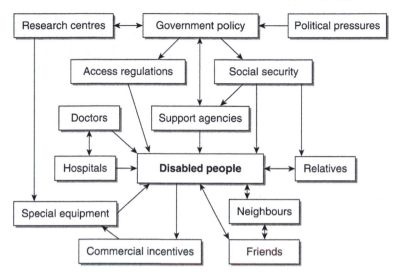

Figure 10.4 Conceptually ordered display

Figure 10.5 Role ordered display

there is an even greater volume of written and visual resources waiting to be interpreted. As would be expected, there is a wide range of analytical methods that can be applied to analysis of the subtleties of texts and visual materials. Both quantitative and qualitative options are available. A distinction can be made between the different aims of the analysis – criticism, interpretation or evaluation.

A critical approach focuses on the technical analysis of the text, examining its integrity within its historical and cultural context. For this you will need to explore the philosophical background by examining the related literature, carefully examine the structure of the argument and evidence on which it is based, possible sources of bias due to the writer's situation, and the clarity of the language in getting the message across.

The art of interpretation, also called **hermeneutics** (Hermes was a messenger of the gods in Greek mythology, famous for his coded messages that needed interpretation), lies in finding out the meanings behind the text (or visual material). The meanings are always based on the perspective of the creator, whether political, philosophical, psychological, feminist, religious, etc. and his or her intentions when writing, i.e. what particular issues were being addressed. And, of course, you will also have your own viewpoint from which you interpret the work. Often with historical documents, not only is the contemporary context of the material of relevance, but there may be insights gained by the subsequent influences that have been caused by it (e.g. Freud's *Interpretation of Dreams*, the Bible, the *Communist Manifesto*).

When you read a text, or look at an illustration you naturally make an evaluation of it – interesting, boring, well written, obscure, etc. This instinctive process can be formalized into a more rigorous process that examines the work from the perspectives of the text, the reader and the context in which evaluation takes place. While this process will always be subjective, different evaluators will differ in their evaluations. There are arguments to be made when examining the work as to its clarity, complexity, integrity, ingenuity, etc. The position and character of the reader (i.e. you) will obviously be influential – your likes and dislikes, literary skills, vested interests, etc. Then the context, what is the purpose of your evaluation? Is it to gauge its suitability for a particular purpose, to compare it with another work, to provide a review (aimed at whom)?

Although these approaches are different in their intentions, you can see that there are obvious links between them that can be integrated into a general assessment of the texts or visual material. It is worth considering now in more detail the techniques that can be employed in qualitative analysis. Here is a brief summary of some of the more common methods.

Interrogative insertion

This method consists of devising and inserting implied questions into a text for which the text provides the answers. In this way, you can uncover the logic (or lack of it) of the discourse and the direction and emphasis of the argument as made by the author. This helps to uncover the recipient design of the text – how the text is written to appeal to a particular audience and how it tries to communicate a particular message.

Problem–solution discourse

This is a further development of interrogative insertion which investigates the implications of statements more closely. Most statements can be read to have one of two implications. This is very commonly found in advertising, e.g. 'Feeling tired? Eat a Mars Bar.' The same, but in a more extended form, is found in reports, instruction manuals and books. The analysis aims to uncover the sequence of the argument by following through first the situation, then the problem, followed by the response and the result and evaluation. The absence of any of these steps in the sequence will lead to a sense of incompleteness and lack of logical argument. Another way of presenting the analysis is to devise a network in the form of a decision tree that traces the problems and the possible solutions, along with their implications.

Membership categorization

This technique analyses the way people, both writers and readers, perceive commonly held views on social organization, how people are expected to behave, how they relate to each other and what they do in different social situations. For example, the relationships between parents and their children, the behaviour of members of different classes of society, or the roles of different people in formal situations. Most of these assumptions are not made explicit in the text. By highlighting what is regarded as normal, assumptions and pre-judgements may be revealed and an understanding of typical characterization can be gained.

Rhetorical analysis

Rhetoric is the use of language and argument to persuade the listener or reader to believe the author. For example, politicians try to give the impression that they should be believed, and harness the vocabulary and structure of spoken and written language to bolster this impression. Rhetorical analysis uncovers the techniques used in this kind of communication. Rhetoric is used to aim at a specific audience or readership. It may appeal to, and engender belief in, the target audience, but is likely to repel and undermine the confidence of others. For example, a racist diatribe will encourage certain elements on the far right, but repel others.

The analysis detects credibility markers – signals that indicate the 'rightness' of the author and the 'wrongness' of others, such as assertions about the 'correct' moral position, claims of privileged understanding and dismissal of alternatives as unbelievable. Even in apparently non-partisan writing, such as scientific reports, where the author is de-personalized, rhetorical techniques are used to persuade the reader about the 'rightness' of the conclusions. Here, one should check for markers relating to objectivity, logic and correct methodology.

Narrative analysis

This form of analysis is aimed at extracting themes, structures, interactions and performances from stories or accounts that people use to explain their past, their present situation or their interpretations of events. The data, which are primarily aural, are collected by semi- or unstructured interviews, participant observation or other undirected methods. The narrative is analysed for different aspects, such as what is said rather than how, or conversely, the nature of the performance during the telling, and perhaps how the storyteller reacted with the listener(s). Alternatively, the structure of the story is inspected. All this is done to reveal the undercurrents that may lie beneath the simple narrative of the story.

Semiotics

This is the term for the 'science of signs', which is used to examine visual and other media as well as written texts. **Semiotics** attempts to gain a deep understanding of meanings by the interpretation of single elements of text or visual units. Words are only meaningful in their relationship with other words, e.g. we only know the meaning of 'horse' if we can compare it with different animals with different features. Likewise, the meanings of objects are related to their context, e.g. the meanings of a red traffic light can be seen as embedded in the system of traffic laws, colour psychology, codes of conduct and convention, etc. (which could explain why for a time in China, a red traffic light meant 'go'). A strong distinction is therefore made between denotation (what we perceive) and connotation (what we read into) when analysing a sign.

A range of technical terms has been devised that indicate the different aspects of signs, for example: 'signifier' – that which performs as a vehicle for the meaning; 'signified' – what the signifier points to; 'denotative meaning' – the obvious functional element of the sign; 'code' or 'sign system' – the generalized meaning instilled in a sign, and many others. This can simply be explained by looking at a traffic sign and attributing these terms to the various parts, as shown in Figure 10.6.

Sign	**Signifier 1. Warning (triangle)**	**Signifier 2. Right bend**

Signified: Warning, right bend ahead

Denotative meaning: Slow down

Code or sign system: National traffic signs

Figure 10.6 The semiotics of a traffic sign

Discourse analysis

Discourse analysis studies the way that people communicate with each other through language within a social setting. Language is not a neutral medium for transmitting information; it is embedded in our social situation and helps to create and recreate it. Language shapes our perception of the world, our attitudes and identities. Two central themes can be identified: the interpretive context in which the discourse is set, and the rhetorical organization of the discourse. The former concentrates on analysing the social context, for example the power relations between the speakers (perhaps due to age or seniority) or the type of occasion where the discourse takes place (a private meeting or at a party). The latter investigates the style and scheme of the argument in the discourse; for example, a sermon will aim to convince the listener in a very different way from a lawyer's presentation in court.

Post-structuralist social theory, and particularly the work of the French theorist Michel Foucault, has been influential in the development of this analytical approach to language. According to Foucault, discourses are 'practices that systematically form the objects of which they speak' (1972: 43). He could thus demonstrate how discourse is used to make social regulation and control appear natural.

Symbolic interaction

Going beyond communication just through discourse, Blumer (1969) maintained that all communication is symbolic and based on interaction and meaning; that is, your interaction with your environment is instrumental in the formation of the meanings you attribute to yourselves, other people and things. This theory of **symbolic interactionism** is founded on three basic components: meaning, language and thought. The meanings that you attribute to people and things are the central aspect to your behaviour. Obviously, every individual will differ in their meanings, and it is through language that people can communicate and negotiate their perspectives via the use of symbols. These symbols are interpreted and modified through thought generated by different points of view revealed through language communication. Your concept of 'self' is then generated by gauging the responses and expectations of the people you communicate with, as it were, by seeing how other people see you.

Using participant observation, interviewing, and analysis of inter-actions and their contexts, it is possible to gain understanding of the way people interact. Misunderstandings and disputes can often be the result of different meanings attributed to matters under discussion or when communicating in some other form or when working together. Harmonious relationships are the result of shared meanings or an appreciation and acceptance of differences.

WHERE TO FIND OUT MORE

As you would expect with this big and complex subject, there are a myriad of books dedicated to explaining all aspects. All the textbooks on social research methods will have sections on qualitative analysis. In the list below, I have tried to explain a bit about the individual book and how it may be of use to you. I have ordered them in a way that I think moves from the simplest to the most sophisticated.

Robson, C. (2015) *Real World Research: A Resource for Social Scientists and Practitioner-Researchers* (fourth edition). Oxford: Blackwell.
A brilliant resource book, and should be used as such. Good for getting more detailed information on most aspects of data collection and analysis. See chapter 18 for analysing and interpreting qualitative data.

Bryman, A. (2015) *Social Research Methods* (fifth edition). Oxford: Oxford University Press.
Another fantastic book on all aspects of social research. Part 3 is about qualitative research.

David, M. and Sutton, C. (2004) *Social Research: The Basics*. London: Sage.
See chapter 16 to start with.

Flick, U. (2014) *An Introduction to Qualitative Research* (fifth edition). London: Sage.
Part 6 deals particularly with analysis of qualitative data.

Seale, C. (ed.) (2011) *Researching Society and Culture* (third edition). London: Sage.
This edited book has chapters by various authors, each on one aspect of research. See those on qualitative analysis, choosing whatever is appropriate for your study.

Seale, C., Gobo, G., Gubrium, J. and Silverman, D. (2006) *Qualitative Research Practice*. London: Sage.
An edited book with chapters by almost 40 leading experts in the field and covering a diversity of methods and a variety of perspectives. Pick the bits that are relevant for you.

For a comprehensive, though incredibly dense and rather technical, guide to qualitative data analysis, refer to:

Miles, M.B. and Huberman, A.M. (2013) *Qualitative Data Analysis: A Methods Sourcebook* (third edition). London: Sage.

This has a lot of examples of displays that help to explain how they work, but is technically sophisticated so you might find it difficult initially to understand the terminology in the examples. To help in this respect, this third edition has a really useful online Student Study Site, with all the materials especially geared towards maximizing your understanding of the material.

And a few more books if you don't find what you want in the above. Your library catalogue will list many more. Try a search using keywords, such as data analysis with management, education (or whatever your particular subject is), to see if there are specific books dedicated to your particular interest.

Silverman, D. (2015) *Interpreting Qualitative Data* (fifth edition). London: Sage.

This has new material on doing qualitative research online and the ethics of Internet research. It provides plenty of study examples drawn from a broad range of disciplines including business, education, social work and geography as well as health studies. It offers a website too.

Holliday, A. (2016) *Doing and Writing Qualitative Research* (third edition). London: Sage.

A general guide to writing qualitative research aimed at students of sociology, applied linguistics, management and education.

Schwandt, T. (2015) *Qualitative Enquiry: A Dictionary of Terms* (fourth edition). Thousand Oaks, CA: Sage.

To help you understand all the technical jargon.

Coffey, A. and Atkinson, P. (1996) *Making Sense of Qualitative Data: Complementary Research Strategies*. London: Sage.

A bit dated, but the authors take an unusual approach by taking a single data set, which they analyse using a number of techniques to highlight the range of approaches available to qualitative researchers.

Griffin, E., Ledbetter, A. and Spark, G. (2014) *A First Look at Communication Theory* (ninth edition). Columbus, OH: McGraw-Hill Education.

This introduces 32 diverse theories about communication that are a mix of foundational and recent scholarship and, with the benefit of numerous examples and connections to pop culture, will help you to apply them to your own life! It promises to provide a solid foundation for an understanding of the relationships between theories. Chapter 5 is about symbolic interactionism; chapter 26 is about semiotics.

11

MIXED METHODS AND
INTERDISCIPLINARY RESEARCH

MIXED METHODS

The almost definitive distinction between quantitative/positivist and qualitative/relativist research methods is neat and simplistic, but rather goes against our normal experience of life, where quantity and quality are usually considered to be different but complementary aspects of the same phenomenon. Why not use a variety of methods when doing a research project? Apparently, it is not as simple as that. You would hardly believe it from the usually sober world of researchers that, according to Densin (2010) there have been three 'wars' about just this subject since the 1970s! The problem revolved around the issue of paradigm assumptions – the relationship between paradigm, methodology, epistemology and ethics. Consequently, even agreeing on a definition of mixed methods research is problematic. There is not the space here to go into great detail about the disputes (see Densin's paper for this, and if you want more, see Symonds and Gorard (2008), Sale, Lohfeld and Brazil (2002) and Yanchar and Williams (2006)). To summarize, the three stages in the quarrel, in Densin's words, are:

> The post-positivist war against positivism (1970–1990); the wars between competing post-positivist, constructivist, and critical theory paradigms (1990–2005); and the current war between evidence-based methodologists and mixed methods, interpretive and critical theory schools (2005 to present).

As indicated above, there were some experts who maintained that the philosophical basis of quantitative and qualitative research are so different (i.e. positivism and relativism) that you cannot combine the two approaches in one study, the so-called incompatibility thesis (Hughes and Sharrock, 1997; Smith, 1983). But it is now fairly generally accepted that the distinction between the methods used for quantitative and qualitative research are not as distinct as previously believed, that many data collection methods and data types can be used for both approaches and that the paradigms behind them can coexist in a single study (Symonds and Gorard, 2008). In fact, mixed methods has quite recently become recognized as the third possible approach to research, in addition to quantitative and qualitative (Tashakkori and Teddlie, 2003). Far from clashing with the different philosophical bases of quantitative and qualitative methodologies, mixed methods welcomes the differences and acts to combine them in different ways in order to gain extra breadth and depth of understanding.

So much interest is there in this developing way of doing research, that, according to Onwuegbuzie (2012), there are currently thirty-one published books, hundreds of papers, and several conferences and online groups devoted to doing mixed methods research.

In this chapter, I will chart a course between these disputes to provide some practical advice on how to do mixed methods research and I will also discuss the advantages of looking at complex phenomena in a variety of ways by using different methods. With this combination, you can either delve deeper than is possible with only one approach or to explore how this can be related to the concept of **triangulation,** which is the technique of examining a phenomenon from different points of view in order to cross-check the results of the investigations. These can help to make stronger arguments for your interpretation of the evidence and lead to more robust conclusions.

So, let's start with a few definitions of mixed methods research in order to understand what we are discussing here. Johnson, Onwuegbuzie and Turner (2007) include nineteen different definitions provided by leading researchers. The most compact of these were by:

> John Creswell: . . . *a research design or methodology in which the researcher collects, analyses and mixes (integrates or connects) both quantitative and qualitative data in a single study or a multiphase program of enquiry*

> Hallie Preskill: . . . *refers to the use of data collection methods that collect both quantitative and qualitative data. Mixed methods research acknowledges that all methods have inherent biases and weaknesses; that*

using a mixed method approach increases the likelihood that the sum of data collected will be richer, more meaningful, and ultimately more useful in answering the research questions.

Michael Q. Patten: *. . . enquiring into a question using different data sources and design elements in such a way as to bring different perspectives to bear on the inquiry and therefore support triangulation of the findings. In this way, using different methods to examine different questions in the same overall study is not mixed methods.*

And one that is rather more expansive:

Udo Kelle: *. . . the combination of different qualitative and quantitative methods of data collection and data analysis in one empirical research project. This combination can serve for two different purposes: it can help to discover and to handle threats for validity arising from the use of qualitative or quantitative research by applying methods from the alternative methodological tradition and can thus ensure good scientific practice by enhancing the validity of methods and research findings. Or it can be used to gain a fuller picture and deeper understanding of the investigated phenomenon by relating complementary findings to each other which result from the use of methods from the different methodological traditions of qualitative and quantitative research.*

WHY TO DO MIXED METHODS RESEARCH

The reasons for using mixed methods can be listed as follows:

- to explain and interpret a situation;
- to explore a phenomenon;
- to develop and test a new instrument;
- to serve a theoretical perspective;
- to complement the strengths of a single design;
- to overcome the weaknesses of a single design;
- to address a question at different levels;
- to address a theoretical perspective at different levels.

GUIDELINES FOR METHOD USE

With the whole range of research methods available for mixing and matching in your project, how do you make a selection that is suitable for your project and which makes sense in the context of your research? In order to provide some orientation through the multiple opportunities provided by mixed methods research, Yanchar and Williams (2006) proposed five guidelines aimed at ensuring that you develop a defensible programme of enquiry. In brief these consist of:

1   **contextual sensitivity** – tailor your choice of research methods to the demands of the particular research questions and their context;
2   **creativity** – be imaginative in the construction of theories, formulation of questions and problem solving, using a creative combination of suitable research methods rather than adopting some unsuitable standardized formula;
3   **conceptual awareness** – acknowledge that all aspects of your work are based on philosophical standpoints, no research subject is historically unburdened and lacking in individual theoretical bases;
4   **coherence** – select methods that are compatible to produce meaningful and interpretable accounts, and which are based on an overall theoretical purpose that avoids contradiction and self-refutation;
5   **critical reflection** – identify and evaluate the consequences of assumptions and values that underlie the research questions and chosen research methods.

'MIXING' METHODS CAN BE DONE IN DIFFERENT WAYS

One way of categorizing ways of doing mixed methods research is to gauge the balance between the quantitative and qualitative elements of the project (Johnson, Onwuegbuzie and Turner, 2007):

*   **qualitative dominant** – based primarily on a constructivist-post-structuralist-critical approach with the addition of quantitative methods where appropriate;
*   **equal status** – a pragmatic approach that sees qualitative and quantitative research as compatible and complementary;
*   **quantitative dominant** – based on a post-positivist quantitative approach, while recognizing that some qualitative aspects are usefully studied.

Whichever balance you use will depend on the subject of your study and your comfort level of working with quantitative and/or qualitative data. But it is not only the balance of these two perspectives that you need to decide on, it is also the strategies that you will employ in their use. Clark and Creswell (2008) have a useful summary of the different sequential or concurrent use of the different methods:

- sequential explanatory
- sequential exploratory
- sequential transformative
- concurrent triangulation
- concurrent nested
- concurrent transformative.

It is worth exploring these in a little more detail and illustrating them with short examples to give a more practical view of how they can be used.

- **sequential explanatory** – this is where you first collect and analyse quantitative data, and then use qualitative methods to further explain and interpret the results and promote generalizability.

  example – a questionnaire survey was carried out to find out how many people with children in a housing development used which nearby play and sports facilities, and the main reasons for doing so. The quantitative data analysis found that there was a significant difference of use between certain groups of people. A round of qualitative interviews was undertaken to find out in more detail (explain) what the reasons for these differences were, using the data from the questionnaire responses to set up the variables to be explored, allowing more to come forward through open questions during the conversations;

- **sequential exploratory** – is the opposite way around to the previous method, where you start with qualitative methods and use the results to set up the quantitative part of the study.

  example – in order to discover the main beliefs and customs that immigrants from Eritrea followed and how these conflicted with those of their host country, an exploratory series of discussion groups were held with newly arrived and longer-term immigrants.

The data gathered from these discussions were used to formulate the concepts and variables for a questionnaire survey to provide statistical analysis of the nature and scale of the problems;

- **sequential transformative** – here, both quantitative and qualitative methods are used, one after the other, and only when the results are achieved are they integrated and interpreted in a complementary fashion, making use of the strengths of each for different aspects of the study.

    example – a questionnaire survey was carried out to discover how many people in contrasting urban and rural areas preferred to buy organic produce and why, using closed questions to assess the scale of their preferences and the main reasons for their choices. A series of open-ended interviews were held with a sample of people from each area, exploring the same subject. The results of both analyses were combined to provide a rich picture of the comparative levels of preferences and the main reasons behind them, as well as detailed accounts of attitudes and motivations of individual people to explain their choices;

- **concurrent triangulation** – the two approaches are deliberately used equally, at the same time, in order to cross-check (i.e. triangulate) the various findings, and to optimize the data collection and analysis tasks.

    example – a new, innovative, foreign language course was introduced in a language school, and the owners of the school wanted to decide whether to adopt it. A multi-method approach was undertaken in order to gauge the outcomes after it had been used for a year and to compare these with the conventional course. Quantitative data from the results of tests and exams were compared and students were consulted about their experiences during the courses and asked to provide reasons why they thought they achieved the results they did. The teachers were also asked about the ease of delivery of the two courses and their opinion about the reasons behind the level of achievement gained. The results gave the owners a multi-perspective overview of the level of success and popularity of the new course;

- **concurrent nested** – either the qualitative or quantitative approach is given priority and guides the project, and the remaining approach is embedded within the process so that specific questions can be answered.

example – a design team wanted to develop a new electric golf buggy. In order to decide on the dimensions and technical specification of the vehicle, data were collected on the range of sizes and weights of golfers, their equipment, the terrain that the buggy was expected to negotiate and the possible options to power it. At the same time, potential buyers were asked about their stylistic preferences so that the design could be made to look attractive;

- **concurrent transformative** – this involves using the appropriate research design for each of the research questions.

  example – the main research question was about how to organize a water supply to new squatter settlements in a fast-growing city in a developing country. Sub-questions focused on four different aspects of the problem: economic, political, technical and social. Appropriate data collection and analysis methods were used to answer each sub-question (e.g. quantitative to gauge the economic challenges; qualitative to establish the political awareness and capability for coping; quantitative to assess the required technical specifications; and qualitative to explore user perspectives). The findings from each were amalgamated to answer the main research question.

DATA MANAGEMENT AND MIXING

The whole point of doing mixed methods research is to widen the sources and types of data that can be collected in order to provide a richer resource for analysis. Although this can provide great breadth of perspective around a particular subject of study, it can be more labour intensive and time-consuming than using a single method. It also requires you to have multiple skills in the different methods and when and how they are used, something that can be of advantage in your future work. A good system of management is required to cope with the organization of various activities and types of data.

For the reader, it is important to provide a clear rationale of why and how you made the choices of methods and the functions that each has performed. You should describe each system of data collection and analysis and where and how you have integrated them. Any problems of compatibility or limitations that you experienced on the way should be reported, and, more positively, point out the extra insights that you gained from integrating or combining the methods. All this will ensure that you demonstrate rigour in carrying out the research, which in turn will strengthen the credibility of your findings and conclusions.

INTERDISCIPLINARY RESEARCH

Many subjects cut across the conventional disciplinary boundaries that are a feature of branches of learning, such as natural science, social studies, the humanities, and the disciplines within these, e.g. biology and physics, education and healthcare, and within disciplines themselves, e.g. experimental maths and applied maths – I am sure you can add many more from your own experience. The main problem encountered with combining disciplines in one research study is that the underlying perspectives and theoretical foundations are often very different. Just as with combining research methods, a way has to be found to enable varied approaches to be linked, reconciled or even merged. It is no doubt easier to combine the disciplines that lie closer together than those with completely different skill sets.

Note that there is a distinction between interdisciplinarity and multi-disciplinarity, where the former seeks to integrate and/or synthesize perspectives from several disciplines, and the latter works through coop-eration between the disciplines, but each works within its own standard frameworks (Barry, Born and Weszkalnys, 2008). The same authors note that the main drivers to interdisciplinarity are both industry and govern-ment, which expect 'research to bring science and technology closer to the needs and concerns of citizens and consumers, reducing the risks of public resistance, uninformed criticism or indifference and stoking the engines of innovation'. They add that there is a growing awareness that many issues are unavoidably multifaceted, such as climate change, GM crops, nuclear power, globalization, the IT industry, etc.

The skills required by a good interdisciplinary researcher are based on an open-minded attitude that embraces new ideas, is flexible, open to change, creative and good at team working, with a willingness to listen and the ability to communicate. A high tolerance to ambiguity is also required to keep options open and to allow new explorations across boundaries (Tait and Lyall, 2007).

Interdisciplinary projects should start with an open-ended preliminary research phase to explore the range of the project in order to determine possible boundaries and to decide which disciplines are most relevant to the questions raised. Tait and Lyall (2007) list what the outcomes of this exploratory phase should be:

• a specification of the range of issues that are central to the research problem;
• how they interact with one another to create or sustain the problem;
• how these interactions can be modified to deliver an implementable, synergistic solution.

They add that extra effort is required on the part of the research team to promote cohesion through combining expertise and overcoming communication problems, resolving divergences in worldviews across disciplines, as well as coordinating institutional structures and procedures. A management structure should be devised to ensure that the projected outcomes can be achieved. A description of this preliminary research phase should be included in the research proposal to provide evidence that a cohesive strategy has been adopted.

In praise of interdisciplinary work and the rewards it can bring, Nissani (1997) suggests that these fall into three overlapping categories:

1 **growth of knowledge** – promoting creative breakthroughs, bringing in the perspectives of 'outsiders', and generating cross-disciplinary oversights as well as bridging disciplinary gaps and fostering flexibility in research. The ideal of a unity of knowledge is promoted that encompasses the various components of human knowledge;
2 **other social benefits** – complex or practical problems can be understood through a more holistic vision that can be a resource for promoting the improvement of society;
3 **personal rewards** – transgressing conventional subject boundaries is a spur to academic and intellectual freedom.

These should result in making you a more informed, open-minded, multi-skilled and resourceful researcher!

WHERE TO FIND OUT MORE

There are a growing number of books dedicated to explaining mixed methods research methods. Here is a selection that will provide you with more information.

DeCuir-Gunby, J. and Schutz, P. (2017) *Developing a Mixed Methods Proposal: A Practical Guide for Beginning Researchers* (Mixed Methods Research). Thousand Oaks, CA: Sage Publications.

This is a really useful, hands-on guide that helps you to create a mixed methods research proposal for your dissertations, grant, or general research studies. There are plenty of examples from actual studies and a complete proposal at the end of the book. If you complete the exercises in each chapter you will have an individualized, detailed template for your own mixed methods research proposal.

Creswell, J.W. (2014). *A Concise Introduction to Mixed Methods Research*. London: Sage Publications.

This book provides a brief overview of mixed methods research that takes you through the essential steps in planning and designing a study. It offers students and practitioners in the social, behavioral, and health sciences a foundation for understanding mixed methods methodology.

Tashakkori, A. and Teddlie, C. (eds) (2010) *Sage Handbook of Mixed Methods in Social & Behavioral Research* (second edition). Thousand Oaks, CA: Sage Publications.

This is a big book that examines all aspects of mixed methods research across a variety of disciplines. It covers all aspects of inquiry, from conceptualizing research to selecting methods, analysing and interpreting data, and reporting findings. It also provides learning objectives, discussion questions and exercises, and extensive cross-referencing to help you in your studies.

And here are some books aimed at specific disciplines:

Watkins, D. and Gioia, D. (2015). *Mixed Methods Research* (Pocket Guides to Social Work Research Methods). New York: Oxford University Press.

This practical guide to mixed methods research has been written with health and human services professionals in mind. It reviews the fundamentals of mixed methods research designs and the general suppositions of mixed methods procedures, looks critically at mixed methods studies and models that have already been employed in social work, and reflects on the contributions of this work to the field.

Curry, L. and Nunez-Smith, M. (2014). *Mixed Methods in Health Sciences Research: A Practical Primer* (Vol. 1). Thousand Oaks, CA: Sage Publications.

This book pulls together foundational mixed methods principles, synthesizes the knowledge base in the field, and translates it for health science researchers. It presents key theories, concepts, and approaches in an accessible way and is packed with illustrations from the health sciences literature.

Mehdi Riazi, A. (2017) *Mixed Methods Research in Language Teaching and Learning*. Sheffield: Equinox Publishing.
This volume is the first to examine MMR in language teaching and learning and how such a methodology works in practice.

Roelen, K. and Camfield, L. (eds) (2015). *Mixed Methods Research in Poverty and Vulnerability: Sharing Ideas and Learning Lessons*. Basingstoke: Palgrave Macmillan.
This volume shares experiences from research in developed and developing country contexts on how mixed methods approaches can make research more credible, usable and responsive to complexity.

And one on interdisciplinarity:

Repko, A.F., Szostak, R. and Buchberger, M.P. (2017) *Introduction to Interdisciplinary Studies* (second edition). Thousand Oaks, CA: Sage Publications.
This book shows a different way of thinking that can lead to new solutions for complex real-world problems. It breaks down the process of interdisciplinary studies into manageable and understandable parts and is illustrated with plenty of clear examples, interesting analogies and a detailed deconstruction of interdisciplinarity.

12

WRITING THE PROPOSAL AND PLANNING THE RESEARCH PROJECT

Before starting a research programme it is necessary to work out exactly what you want to do, why and how. A research proposal is a succinct summary of just that. Obviously, it will be very helpful to you, the researcher, to make it clear to yourself what the aims of the research are and what you need to do to achieve the desired outcome. It will also be a useful way to inform others of your intentions. In fact, the presentation of a research proposal is always required by courses that contain a research exercise, such as writing a dissertation or a thesis. In professional life, for all research projects that need funding you will be required to provide a detailed research proposal as part of the funding application.

FORMULATING A SUCCESSFUL RESEARCH PROPOSAL

Fortunately, research proposals tend to follow a defined pattern. They all need to explain the nature of the research and its context, and why it is needed. This then prepares the way for a statement of the aims and objectives of the research, how it will be carried out and what the outcomes are likely to be. Then there is a description of what resources will be required (time, money, equipment, staffing, etc.) to carry out the work.

The research proposal, once approved, will act as a contract outlining the basis of agreement between the parties involved; for example, the researcher, supervisors, institutions (e.g. university or college). In funded research, this will be part of a formal signed contract with the providers of the funds, which cannot be substantially altered without the agreement of all parties. It is therefore advisable not to 'promise mountains and deliver molehills'!

In the context of research as an educational exercise, research projects should be suitable vehicles for students to learn and practise the theoretical and methodological aspects of the research process as much as being a way to gain new insights into the subject studied.

THE MAIN INGREDIENTS AND SEQUENCE

Academic research proposals are usually composed of the following elements:

* the title
* aims of the research
* the background to the research – context and previous research
* a definition of the research problem
* outline of methods of data collection and analysis
* possible outcomes
* timetable of the project and description of any resources required
* list of references.

The title

The function of the title is to encapsulate in a few words the essence of the research. Ideally it should contain all the essential keywords that someone might use in an attempt to locate the kind of study you are proposing. These words are likely to include the main concept and variables, and limits to the scope. You can leave out such phrases as 'an investigation into', 'a study of', 'aspects of', as these are obvious attributes of a research project.

Take for example the title, 'The implications of the present Labour and Conservative policies on what is taught in primary schools in England'. The independent variables are 'Labour and Conservative policies', and the dependent variable is 'what is taught'; the type of research task is implied as a comparative study; the theoretical basis is one of prediction of effects of policies; and the purpose of the study is to predict their effects on the curricula of primary schools. Also important are the words that limit the scope of the research, e.g. only 'present policies', only those of 'Labour and Conservatives', only in 'the present', only effects on what is 'taught', only in 'primary schools', and only in 'England'.

Aims of the research

This goes right to the heart of the project. One main aim, and perhaps two or three subsidiary aims resulting from it are sufficient. Precision is essential – too many or vague aims indicate woolly thinking and will be difficult or impossible to achieve within the available resources and time.

The context – background and previous research

This explains to the reader the background from which the research problem emerges. It should explain the major factors which surround your problem, and any significant literature which relates to it. It also has the function of capturing the interest of the reader.

Some of the factors which make up the context might be of a physical nature, such as location, materials, artefacts, organizations, processes, etc. while others might be more conceptual, such as the economy, legislation, development policy, etc. Even more abstract are theoretical concepts such as power, poverty and Marxism. The research problem should emerge from this context.

Virtually every subject has been researched previously, so a critical account of what has been achieved so far to address the problem is required to identify any gaps in knowledge or contentious issues. Accurate referencing is essential here. The research should fill one of these gaps or try to resolve the contention. It is quite difficult to pitch the level of your text so that any intelligent reader understands the factors from which your problem emerges, while at the same time persuading the expert that you are conversant with details of the principal issues. Do not assume that the reader knows anything about your subject.

The research problem

The research problem provides the focus of the research project. It is the culmination of the background work and the initiator of the specific research tasks. It must be very clearly defined to explain the nature of the problem and why it is significant. The problem may be expressed in abstract **terms** initially, but through the statement of **sub-problems**, you should indicate how it can be investigated practically.

Outline of methods

This part of the proposal explains briefly what you are going to do in order to carry out your research, based on your chosen research approach. In proposals for funded research, this may need to be described in great detail.

Every proposal is different in its description of methods, as these have to be specifically tailored to efficiently collect and analyse data relevant to the specific research problem and to produce the outcomes aimed at. One common feature is likely to be a review of the literature relevant to the research topic. It is generally relevant to distinguish between the methods of data collection and data analysis, although in some cases, particularly in qualitative research, these may go hand in hand. The explanation will outline which methods you will use for what, and why. You will probably need to refer to books that describe the methods in detail. There may be only one method used, e.g. experimental, or a combination of several, each suitable for different aspects of the research. You may have to indicate how you will be able to access certain types of information if these are obscure, in remote locations or only available to certain people. Access to materials or equipment may also be discussed.

Possible outcomes of the research

Although you cannot predict exactly what the outcomes will be (if you could, there would be little point in carrying out the research), you should try to be quite precise as to the nature and scope of the outcomes and as to who might benefit from the information. The outcomes should relate directly to the aims of the research. Note that in PhD proposals and most funded research there is a need to indicate what will be the original contribution to knowledge.

Timetable of the project and description of any resources required

There is always a time limit to research projects – particularly strict if it is a piece of university or college coursework. The formulation of a timetable is therefore essential in order to allocate time limits to the sequence of tasks that you need to accomplish to hand the finished report or dissertation in on time. This is not only a test of the practicality of the proposed project, but also an organizational guide when you carry out the work.

Resources that are essential to the project, such as equipment, transport, skills, software, etc. should be listed and availability assured so that you can convince the reader (and yourself) of the practicality of achieving the aims of the project.

List of references

The location of the cited work of others must be meticulously recorded in this list. Not only does this ensure that you cannot be accused of plagiarism, but it also demonstrates that you are aware of the latest thinking in the subject. However, keep the references relevant – it is not a bibliographic list of all the literature surrounding the subject.

WRITING THE PROPOSAL

For a major undertaking, such as a final year dissertation or research degree, it is important to keep conferring with your tutor or supervisor as you refine the structure of the argument and develop your successive drafts of the proposal. Comments from other members of staff and/or colleagues can be useful too, as they might see things from a different perspective. Remember, however, that it is you who must decide what you want to do in the research, so be prepared to discuss it further with your tutor if you do not agree with some of the comments or recommendations made by others.

Why might a proposal be rejected? Here are some reasons:

- There is no need for the research.
- The scale of the proposed research is too big so an adequate conclusion cannot be reached.
- The aims and objectives are vague or impractical or do not match, or are expressed as personal goals.
- The research problem is not clearly defined, so the research work has no adequate focus.
- The procedures are confused with the objectives.
- There is a lack of logic in the argument in the proposal, so the link between the research aims and outcomes is broken.

- The project is formulated on an emotional or a political agenda rather than a factual or a theoretical basis.
- Not enough information is provided about the details of the project.
- Access to information, equipment or other resources is uncertain or impossible.

The completed proposal must conform to the requirements of the course or project in which you are taking part. Normally, there is limited space on the forms, and often you must ensure that your proposal is no longer than can be comfortably fitted onto two sides of A4 paper. This is not easy, but is a very good discipline in writing a dense argument. Where possible, use the references as a shorthand to describe theoretical approaches.

Here is an example of a research proposal that has been prepared by a master's-level student for their dissertation that they wrote over the space of three months during the summer. I have annotated it to point out the features described above.

Research proposal

This proposal was written by Marina Muenchenbach as part of her Research Methods Module in the master's course, Development and Emergency Practice (DEP), at Oxford Brookes University.

Local economy development in humanitarian assistance for transition to development in post-conflict environments

[*Comment: Note how the title introduces the main concepts and defines and limits the scope of the research.*]

The aims of the research

This research aims to investigate possible concepts and tools that add further knowledge to the question of how best Humanitarian Assistance (HA) Programmes during the transition phase from emergency to development can prepare the ground for long-term and sustainable Local Economy (LE) Development by forming partnerships with Local Markets and achieving Win-Win situations based on common interest.

The research specifically addresses the context of conflict affected environments.

[Comment: This section gives the briefest outline of the aims to explain the focus of the research to the reader, and introduces some of the distinctive issues that will be involved.]

Background to the research

The objectives of Humanitarian Assistance are 'to save lives, alleviate suffering and maintain human dignity during and in the aftermath of man-made crises and natural disasters, as well as to prevent and strengthen preparedness for the occurrence of such situations' (IPB, 2003).

The current system of Humanitarian Assistance is composed of Donors, UN agencies, NGOs and the Red Cross and Red Crescent Movement (ALNAP, 2010). In the last decades, Humanitarian Assistance has made considerable progress in conscious building regarding its impact on economies in conflict affected environments and the need to prepare for a smooth transition to development.

In contrast to Humanitarian Assistance, Development Assistance is economy-centred and is provided bilaterally and multilaterally by developed countries, International Financial Institutions (including the Bretton Woods Institutions WB, IMF and WTO), Foreign Direct Investment and the Private Sector.

[Comment: Here, the two main concepts are defined and explained, with a quotation – note the citation – and references to the literature.]

Humanitarian Assistance and Development currently appear 'disjointed' with a sharp change in objectives from the humanitarian to the development phase. By focusing on 'humanitarian' objectives actors may forget that at one point the respective country will strive for development based on economic efficiency criteria. Assistance can thus run the risk to create prolonged dependency or even hinder independent sustainable development.

[Comment: The main research problem that inspired this research is revealed. This provides the reason and focus for the research.]

Coordination of Humanitarian Assistance was improved by the creation of the UN cluster system in 2005. Within the system, the Early Recovery Cluster was given the specific responsibility for promotion of early steps that enable long-term development (UNDP Country Team Pakistan, 2006).

[Comment: This problem has been tackled to some extent.]

Despite successful efforts on various levels, there is still a lack of awareness of Humanitarian Assistance organizations regarding their impact on local markets. Local purchase is usually not defined as a specific objective in programme planning, which often results in internal administrative and logistical procedures that are unfavourable to purchasing or contracting locally. Local Economy actors on the other hand usually do not have the contacts, knowledge or management capacity to successfully advertise their services.

[Comment: However more needs to be done, particularly about a forgotten issue – that of local markets.]

The research focuses on Local Economy Development in Northern Uganda which after over 20 years of violent internal conflict is in the transition to development.

[Comment: This locates the research in a particular area and situation, limiting its scope in order to make it possible to encompass within a short research project.]

Literature review

Three major areas of current research shall be specifically outlined as relevant to the dissertation.

[Comment: Breaking the review down into separate relevant areas helps to give a structure to the review and to focus the literature search to essential issues.]

The Donor Committee for Enterprise Development has made important attempts in shaping the policy debate for Private Sector Development in post-conflict countries. Their review of current literature and practice (DCED, 2008) states that 'in addition, donor countries are increasingly bringing together development, diplomatic and defence efforts in order to achieve both security and development goals. This not only promotes security for developing countries, but also for donor nations themselves'.

[Comment: Commenting on a previous, and no doubt, far more extensive review of the literature, and introducing a short quotation, mines into a wealth of information that can be used later in the research.]

Making Markets Work for the Poor (M4P) is an approach to poverty reduction that donors such as the Department for International

Development (DFID) and the Swiss Agency for Development and Cooperation (SDC) have been supporting over the past few years. The central idea is that the poor are dependent on market systems for their livelihoods (DFID, 2008).

The growing use of Market Mapping and Analysis (Albu, 2010) and Value Chain Analysis (USAID, 2008) is indicative for an evolving acceptance within the Humanitarian Assistance system of the significance of local markets and of local procurement and innovative forms of market-system support.

[Comment: See how the literature is not just listed, but the ideas are extracted to make a relevant point about the proposed research.]

The main current gap in knowledge concerns methods for practical implementation of formulated policies. The intended research will therefore focus on providing an open forum for concerned actors (Humanitarian Assistance, Local Economy and Local Governments) which allows for participatory brainstorming of possible concepts and tools to achieve stipulated goals.

[Comment: Although very brief, this review has hinted at a gap in knowledge that will be addressed by the proposed research. Space permitting, this review of the literature could be much longer to dig deeper into the state of the art of theory and practice in this subject. However, a short proposal like this should concentrate on the main sources – the more extended exploration of the literature can come in the dissertation itself.]

Research problem

The importance of market integrated approaches in Humanitarian Assistance programmes during the transition phase that prepare the ground for long-term and sustainable Local Economy Development (LED) – specifically in the context of conflict affected environments – starts being acknowledged by the Donor community and concerned actors. However, up to date there is a lack of practical concepts and tools that allow efficient implementation of policies.

[Comment: The problem stated in a nutshell. Note the use of the main concepts and their relationships, and the identification of a need for the research.]

Research Questions

1   What is the current impact of HA on economic sectors critical to long-term development?

   a   What percentage of goods, services and labour do HA organizations acquire locally, nationally and internationally?

   b   What percentage of goods, services and labour as delivered by local economy is purchased, contracted or employed by HA organizations?

2   Which sectors or markets offer win-win opportunities? Do some more than others? Agriculture more than construction? Services more than material?

3   How can 'critical' markets be stimulated to allow for greater involvement of Local Economy?

4   Which body, structure, organization is best suited to promote Local Economy Development at a given location? Is there an existing one? Does a new one have to be created? If yes, what should it look like?

5   Which concepts or tools can support LED and increase partnerships (HA – LE)?

6   Is the use of market mapping and analysis applicable to LED?

7   Is the use of action research in partnerships applicable to LED?

[Comment: Devising questions is a good way to break down the main research problem into practically researchable units aimed at finding the answers. The questions provide a sort of task list for the project, hinting at the type of data that are required and how they should be analysed to produce conclusions that answer the questions. Care should be taken to ensure that the questions are all relevant to the main problem. Also ensure that they can practically be answered within the scope of the project, as is the case here. This section is about 'what to do'.]

Methodology

The research will be carried out following participatory action research principles and will be located in Kitgum, Northern Uganda. The area was chosen as one of the major arenas of humanitarian assistance. It is passing from transition to development and security conditions are favourable.

[Comment: This section is about 'how to do it'. A step-by-step approach is a good way to organize the actual research activities, though you may need to introduce times when reiteration takes place.]

The first step in the research will be the formation of a partnership-type research group consisting of representatives of Humanitarian Assistance, Local Economy, Local Government and Researchers.

The Scandinavian model of Participatory Action Research applied in the research is based on the concept of co-generating knowledge between insiders and outsiders on a specific topic of interest (Eden and Levin as cited in Reason and Bradbury, 2001).

[Comment: Some groundwork is usually required to enable the research actions to take place, whether it is collecting material and equipment, organizing people, or getting the requisite permissions.]

Subsequent steps in the research consist of:

- Data collection of the existing organizational situation from records and interviews with experts, using flowcharts to record the flow of funds, expertise and relationships and interactions in the process of Participatory Action Research.
- Identification of 2 to 3 markets with potential growth potential for LED by interviews with local businesses and market leaders.
- Mapping of identified markets using market mapping to chart key infrastructure, inputs and market-support services; market actors and their linkages in the market chain; and the institutions, rules, norms and trends of the market environment.
- Analysis of collected data using data display and reduction techniques for qualitative data to identify main themes and trends, and descriptive statistics for quantitative data, all aimed at answering the research questions.
- Formulation of Conclusions and Recommendations.

All steps should be carried out under supervision and with the direct involvement of local actors and under supervision of the research group.

[Comment: It is usually far easier to describe the data collection process, as this is a familiar everyday activity, such as asking questions, reading publications and making observations. More difficult, and sometimes

even glossed over in the first proposal drafts, is the ways used to analyse the data collected. The analysis methods are less familiar and need to be learnt about, such as statistical analysis, coding and mapping etc. This is where you will need to consult research methods books to find out what the appropriate analytical methods are for your research. The description here of the analytical methods is rather brief.]

Potential outcomes and limitations to the research

Potential outcomes may consist of agreed recommendations – if possible formulated as programme proposals – that can be adopted by interested actors for future implementation.

[Comment: Although you will not know the answers yet to your research questions, it is good to form an idea of the form of the outcomes and how they might be used.]

The main limitation of the research relates to the scope of work that can be covered within the dissertation period. The study will take place only in one location. Preferably, the described process should be implemented in all main districts of Northern Uganda (Gulu, Amuru, Pader, and Karamoja).

[Comment: No research project can provide all the answers, so it is good to be aware of the limitations of the project so as not to overstate the case when it comes to the conclusions and recommendations. Any contribution to knowledge, however small, is welcome!]

During the initial sourcing donor organizations expressed potential interest in dissemination of results and recommendations within their respective organizations and areas of work.

[Comment: A good point is made here. In order for the findings of your research to be noticed and used, it has to be disseminated in some way to those who will find it interesting or useful.]

The importance of the research – even if limited in scope and location – lies in its practical approach involving existing real actors and its potential to produce applicable concepts and tools that have been developed and agreed by a wider forum.

[Comment: A good way to round off the proposal – stressing the worthwhile nature of the research effort.]

LED Northern Uganda	April		May					June				July					August			
Week	1	2	3	4	5	6	7	8	9	10	11	12	13	14	15	16	17	18	19	20
Calendar week	15	16	17	18	19	20	21	22	23	24	25	26	27	28	29	30	31	32	33	34
Setting the ground																				
Initial sourcing of interests																				
Assessment report																				
Design questionnaire																				
Design google groups																				
Literature review draft																				
Background draft																				
Field research																				
Form research group																				
Data collection for matrices																				
Data analysis/pie charts																				
Decision critical markets											◆									
Market mapping 1																				
Market mapping 2																				
Analysis market mapping																				
Brainstorm concepts and tools																				
Formulate concepts and tools														◆						
Test/pilot concept or tool																				
Evaluate pilot																				
Formulate recommendations																◆				
Workshops research group																				
Dissertation																				
Data collection & analysis																				
Findings, conclusions & recommendations																				
Introduction, methodology etc.																				
Formatting, abbr. references etc.																				
Editing																				
Final presentation & submission																				

Figure 12.1 Outline programme of work

Outline programme of the work

[Comment: An essential part of the research planning is the programme that demonstrates that all the work can be completed before the deadline. When you devise this, it will become clear whether your ambitions match your resources! See figure 12.1.]

List of abbreviations

ALNAP	Active Learning Network for Accountability and Performance
BMZ	Bundesministerium fuer Zusammenarbeit/Federal Ministry for Cooperation
DCED	Donor Committee for Enterprise Development
DEV	Development Economic Cooperation and Development
FIAS	Foreign Investment Advisory Service
GTZ	Deutsche Gesellschaft für Technische Zusammenarbeit
HA	Humanitarian Assistance
	Humanitarian Action
LE	Local Economy
LED	Local Economy Development
LG	Local Government
NGO	Non Governmental Organizations
SDC	Swiss Department for Cooperation
UN	United Nations
UNDP	United Nations Development Program
USAID	United States Agency for International Development.

[Comment: Not always necessary, but in this case this list is really useful in a world filled with acronyms such as the field of international aid and development.]

List of references

Albu, M. (2010) The Emergency Market Mapping and Analysis Toolkit. London: Practical Action Publishing.

ALNAP (2010) The state of the humanitarian system: Assessing performance and progress. London: Oversees Development Institute.

DCED (2008) Private Sector Development in post-conflict countries. A review of current literature and practice. UK: Cambridge. Retrieved on 10 March 2010 from: www.enterprise-development.org.

Del Costello, G. (2008) Rebuilding War-Torn States. The Challenge of Post-Conflict Economic Reconstruction. Oxford: University Press.

DFID (2008) The Operational Guide for the Making Markets Work for the Poor (M4P) Approach. Bern: SDC Distribution Centre.

GTZ, FIAS (2008) Economic Development in conflict-affected countries. (Practitioners' Note.) Eschborn: W.B. Druckerei.

GTZ (2009) Sustainable Economic Development in Conflict-Affected Environments. A Guidebook. Eschborn: W.B. Druckerei.

IPB (2003) Principles and Good Practice of Humanitarian Donorship. Retrieved on 21 March from: http://www.ipb.org/disarmdevelop/.

Reason, P. and Bradbury, H. (2001) Handbook of action research. London: Sage Publications.

UNDP Country Team Pakistan (2006) South Asia Earthquake: Transition from Relief to Development. Retrieved on 21 March from: www.undp.org/.

USAID (2008) Value Chain tools for market-integrated relief: Haiti's construction sector. Retrieved on 12 Feb 2010 from http:// www. microlinks.org/ev02.php?ID=23118_201&ID2=DO_TOPIC.

[Comment: There are strict rules governing the details of how to format lists of references, such as the Harvard System. Find out which system you should comply with. Apart from correct formatting, the main requirements are the accuracy and completeness of the information. Note that this list refers to some citations that do not appear in this extract.]

PLANNING THE PROJECT

One of the components of a research proposal is the project plan or programme. This lists the series of tasks that need to be undertaken and the times that they will require to be completed. For a good example of a programme for a master's dissertation, see the one produced by Marina Muenchenbach in her proposal above.

In order to give realistic timings for carrying out the tasks, especially when fieldwork is involved, you will need to take into account the time needed for travelling, finding willing respondents, chasing up responses, making appointments with busy people, getting permissions and access to archives. If you need special equipment or facilities (e.g. for doing experiments or specialized surveys or tests), ensure that you can get access to these at the necessary times, or adjust your programme to accommodate the availability. All this needs some preliminary investigations and careful consideration of what is practically necessary to complete the tasks. For bigger projects, such as

MPhil or PhD, make sure that you leave plenty of time for revisions after submission of the first full draft to your supervisors. For team projects, build in time for management, meetings, responses from team members, and review procedures. Note also that tasks frequently overlap and that feedback loops are frequently necessary as you gain skills and knowledge. If you use a more sophisticated project planning programme, you can track a critical path through the project that makes clear the essential sequence of tasks, i.e. those that you need to complete before you go on to the next.

Use the programme during the duration of the project to check on your progress. If you overrun on a task, you will be able to make adjustments to the remaining programme so that you do not run out of time at the end. For some tasks, there is a temptation to carry on indefinitely because there is so much to find out and it is so interesting or enjoyable. Your time allocation will bring healthy reality to the situation and rein you in!

It is all very well to plan how long you need for each task, but how much time do you actually have? I mean not so much what is the duration of the project, but how much of your time can you allocate to doing the work? We all have commitments apart from doing the research: personal, professional, other studies, leisure, family, etc. How many hours are available on which days? Is there a regular pattern you can establish, or do you need to do the work in concentrated sessions? And how predictable is your lifestyle? You might need to add in extra time to accommodate unexpected but possible events, such as periods of illness or family affairs. Take all these into account when you do your programme.

WHERE TO FIND OUT MORE

There are books that are solely dedicated to writing academic proposals of all kinds. Some go into great detail, but you will undoubtedly find something useful. I have put them in order of complexity, simplest first. Every book on how to do dissertations will also have a section on writing a proposal.

Locke, L. and Spirduso, W. and Silverman, S. (2013) *Proposals that Work: A Guide for Planning Dissertations and Grant Proposals* (sixth edition). London: Sage.

The publishers claim that previous editions of this book have helped well over 100,000 students and professionals write effective proposals for dissertations and grants. In the fifth edition, the authors have included a discussion of the effects of new technologies and the Internet on the proposal process, with URLs listed where appropriate. The book includes a number of specimen proposals.

Punch, K. (2016) *Developing Effective Research Proposals* (third edition). London: Sage.
A straightforward and helpful guide with a good collection of examples of proposals to illustrate the qualities looked for, organized around three central themes: what is a research proposal, who reads proposals and why? How can you go about developing a proposal? What might a finished proposal look like?

Vithal, R. and Jansen, J. (2012) *Designing Your First Research Proposal: A Manual for Researchers in Education and the Social Sciences* (second edition). Cape Town: Juta.
From selecting a focus to presenting a solid conclusion, this practical, application-centred handbook offers step-by-step instructions on how to write a proposal for basic and advanced research projects.

And here is one written by me:

Walliman, N. (2011) *Your Research Project: Designing and Planning your Work* (third edition). London: Sage.
This is aimed more at PhD- or MPhil-level students, and aims to lead you through the process of formulating a proposal and getting started with the work.

In addition to these specialist books, all of the 'big' research method books will have a section on preparing a proposal and planning the work.

13

WRITING UP THE RESEARCH

If you have produced a well-thought-through proposal and a realistic programme of work, doing the research should be a relatively straight-forward process. However, there is one important organizational task you must complete before you start doing the research, which will ensure that writing up will not be a frustrating experience. This is to devise your system for taking, storing and retrieving notes.

ORGANIZING YOUR NOTES

You will be making hundreds of notes on the literature that you read – books, papers, articles and the web pages that you consult – the bigger the project, the more notes. These notes will be your reservoir of information, an essential resource for writing your report. They will be needed to get you familiar with the state of the art and approaches to research in your subject, writing your literature review, deciding on, describing and carrying out your research methods, and for comparing your results with those of others. Not surprisingly, using an efficient and reliable note taking method, storage and retrieval system will save you a great deal of time and frustration throughout the project. Many hours and days have been wasted by students vainly trying to find that essential quote noted down some months ago and lying somewhere in a pile of papers!

The old-fashioned system was to write your notes onto postcard-size cards which were then headed by a keyword or author's name and filed in boxes in some kind of order. On each card was all the essential citation information about the publication source, and the note was limited to one topic. Hence there could be many cards from the same publication, each on a different topic. Even now, many students start off with making notes in notebooks or file pages in folders, but this soon becomes unwieldy. Writing the reference information on each note is laborious and prone to mistakes. Even those that set up a system of files in their word processor or database programs face the problem of creating efficient organization and retrieval methods.

Dedicated referencing programs have now superseded cards and ad hoc systems, but the principle remains the same. In order to retrieve notes on a particular subject, they should be organized to make this possible by keyword search, and the source of each note must be indicated. There is a wide choice of bibliographic programs that take all the organizational effort out of managing notes and referencing, e.g. ProCite, EndNote, Zotero and many others. Your university or college is likely to favour one of these and provide training and support on its use. If not, before you buy a program, you can search 'comparison of reference management software' on the Internet to make your selection. Some programs are free, some are web based, so accessible anywhere, others are desktop based. You can even use some on your mobile phone or tablet.

Instead of cards, these programs provide template forms into which you insert all the reference information, keywords and your notes. Any number of forms can be compiled, so to make retrieval more efficient, keep the notes on each form strictly dedicated to the one subject indicated by the keyword. When searching for literature, most programs are linked to library catalogues, databases, Google Scholar, etc. that enable you to do searches and to download all the reference information in many standard formats (up to 5,000 styles!) without having to type them out – this really prevents mistakes which are so easily made with the complicated formatting rules! You can often download PDFs, annotate them, and even archive web pages.

A most convenient feature is that many also link with word processing programs such as Microsoft Word, Google Docs, Open Office, etc. so that you can 'cite while you write'. This is particularly useful when retrieving your references – citations and lists of references are automatically generated and inserted in your text.

As usual, don't forget to back up your files. Retrieving notes is easy. You can select them by keyword, author, date, etc. whichever is more useful for your purposes. Obviously, unlike notes written on paper, they are immediately available for pasting, editing and arranging into the first draft of your dissertation text.

MAKING THE BEST USE OF YOUR SUPERVISOR

Although your research project is an exercise in independent study, you will normally be allocated a supervisor to act as a mentor. Depending on your level of study and the way your course is organized you will have access to expert advice to help you to produce your best possible work. Don't think that you can only talk to your supervisor if you have completed your work or are certain about the way ahead. His/her role is to act as a sounding-board for your ideas and to suggest ways to progress your project. In order to make optimum use of your supervisor, find out how much time he/she has allocated to individual students and what arrangements there are for consultations and reviews of your work. You can then plan when are the best times to see him/her. Do stick to your appointment time and keep an eye on the clock to ensure that you can discuss all the issues you want to raise. Make notes on advice and next suggested steps. You can use these notes as a checklist for action and review of progress.

It is always best to send a piece of written work to your supervisor some time before you meet to provide a focus for the discussion. The piece, early on, could be some ideas for your subject, some possible research questions, a draft proposal or a draft literature review. Later you might want to suggest a thesis structure, suitable research methods, or discuss practical issues of gaining data or analysing it. Find out whether there are procedures for reviewing the final draft of the dissertation before submission. You will have to allow time for your supervisor to read through your work and make comments, and then time for you to make any suggested changes or revisions. At PhD stage, in particular, this can be a fairly lengthy process.

WRITING UP A DISSERTATION OR RESEARCH PROJECT

One of the skills essential to successful research is that of writing. Good communication is required at every stage of the project, but the main writing tasks are located at the beginning and end of the research project – at the beginning to explain what you will do in the research, and at the end to explain what you have done and what you have found out. The task is made much easier these days with the help of word processing packages, which provide simple ways to record, store, edit, expand and condense text and to present it in an attractive fashion

If you are doing an undergraduate dissertation or final year project, this will probably be the first lengthy piece of independent writing you undertake. For master's and research degree students, it is the much larger scale and timespan that is the novel element. The main issue when faced with such a task is how to structure the work so that it forms an integral whole. This structure will guide the reader as well as providing a framework to fill in as you are writing. In academic writing, the aim is not to tell a story as one might in a novel, but to set up an argument to support a particular view. You will be trying to persuade the reader that what you have done is worthwhile and based on some kind of logical intellectual process.

Whatever your subject, there must be a central issue that is being investigated which provides the focal point of the text. The body of the dissertation will then revolve around this focal point, perhaps considering it from different perspectives, or examining causes or finding explanations. You will have to come to some conclusions at the end, and this is why argument is required. These conclusions should be based on evidence, and a reasoned argument from this evidence leads to your conclusions.

When to start writing up

It is a daunting prospect to sit down in front of a blank computer monitor with the task of writing a 20,000-, or, in the case of some PhDs, 100,000-word assignment. Thankfully, you can easily avoid this situation. First, you will need to prepare a structure for the writing as soon as you are clear about what you will be doing, probably after you have completed your proposal. The trick then is to gradually amass a collection of notes, observations and data on the issues relevant to your study, which you can then use as a basis for your first draft. The structure will provide a framework into which you can insert your notes. This way, you will have started writing without even realizing it! Don't expect either the framework or the text to be the final version. Both will need refining and revising as your work and understanding progress. Luckily, word processors make revision very quick and easy.

Frame and fill

The framework for your dissertation is most easily created by making a list of possible chapter or section headings. Consult your proposal and plan of work for indications of what these may be. At the very simplest level, the divisions may be like this:

- introduction
- background and previous research
- the main issues and research problem
- research methods – how you will investigate the problem
- a description of the research actions and their results
- conclusions in relation to the research problem.

This is a conventional format, which can be applied to a study in almost any subject. If you want to use an unusual structure or even to develop your own, discuss this with your supervisor to check that it will be acceptable. Once you have the main framework, you can elaborate on the contents of each section by inserting sub-headings to identify the various aspects that you want to consider in each. You will be able to re-order, expand or change these as you progress. However, you will need to know what number of words your assignment should contain so that you can decide how long each section should be to get a balanced result.

You don't have to fill in your text starting from the beginning and proceeding to the end. Use what notes you have so far and insert them where they are relevant within the framework. This way, you will quickly have several pages of (very) rough draft. Although the text will be no more than a series of raw notes, completely unedited, disjointed and incomplete, it will provide you with a solid basis for working on to produce a first draft.

How do you find your notes and get them into the right place? This is where your retrieval techniques will be put to the test. Assuming that your framework gives you enough indication of what you are looking for, search through your notes by keyword or subject. If you do this on the computer, you will be shown a selection of relevant notes, from which you can choose what you think is suitable for that section. You can do this manually with notes on paper. Other useful search parameters may be date or author.

Research methods and data collection and analysis chapters

A good guide to writing the section where you describe the research methods you have used and the reasons for selecting these, is to imagine that the reader will want to repeat your investigations and will look for instructions on to how to do this. In natural science subjects, this is absolutely the function of this section – the experiments or other actions should be repeatable elsewhere to test the reliability of the methods and results. So, be sufficiently precise in your descriptions of the practical steps that you undertook to gain data and analyse them.

The whole point of collecting data and analysing them is that you can come to some conclusions that are relevant to your research problem and achieve the aims of your project. This demanding and creative process requires a lot of clear thinking, perception and meticulous care to build up a logical argument. All the previous work will be devalued if you do not sufficiently draw out the implications of your analysis and capitalize on the insights these afford. You cannot rely on the reader to make inferences from your results. It really is up to you to vividly explain how the results of your analysis provide evidence for new insight into your chosen subject, and respond to the particular research problem that you exposed at the beginning of the research.

A good way to ensure that what you are describing is relevant to your research is to base your chapters on finding the answers to the research questions achieving your aims and objectives. Keeping these in the forefront of your, and your reader's, mind ensures that you only include material that is relevant to your argument. At the end of each section or chapter, summarize the findings and conclusions from each issue studied.

Coming to your main conclusions

Coming to conclusions is a cumulative process. It is unlikely that the problem you have chosen is simple, with questions raised that can be answered with a simple yes or no. Normally, you will find that the questions have several sub-questions requiring individual investigation and answers. Throughout the analysis part of your work you should come to conclusions about these fragments of the main issues. The skill is to gather these up at the end in the concluding chapter to fit them together into a 'mosaic' that will present the complete picture of the conclusion to the entire research project. Just as you should be able to summarize the main problem that your project addresses in one or two sentences, so you should be able to state the conclusion equally briefly.

Revisions

The useful thing about using a word processor is that you can easily change things after you have written them. This takes the pressure off getting everything right first time – something that is impossible to do anyway. Once your work is on paper, then you can review it, get a second opinion on it, and discuss it. You cannot do these if it is still all in your head. Hence the importance of getting on with writing as soon as possible. Regard revisions as an integral part of the process of doing a dissertation. You will of course have to include some time for this in your time plan.

Revision can be done at different levels. The more general levels are concerned with getting the structure and sequence right. At a more detailed level, you might look at the sequence of paragraphs – does each concentrate on one point? Do they follow each other in the right sequence? At the most detailed level you will be looking at grammar, punctuation, vocabulary and spelling.

It is important to keep a track of your revisions, making sure you know what the latest one is! The best way is to save your revision as a new file, clearly labelled with a revision number (e.g. Chapter 3/1, 3/2 etc.). You will thus be able to go back to a previous revision if you change your mind or want to check on some detail. Most word processing programs also provide a facility for keeping track of revisions.

HOW TO WRITE AN ABSTRACT

When you have finished writing your dissertation, thesis, paper or report, you should supply an abstract or executive summary at the beginning to provide potential readers with a very short and concise precis of what your work is about. This is a very important feature, as it will be used on its own in catalogues and online databases to provide information about your publication. You will have noticed yourself when you conduct searches for relevant papers and other publications, how useful the abstracts are to ascertain whether the contents are what you are looking for before you go to the trouble of downloading or buying the publication and reading it in full.

Writing an abstract is a real exercise in concision. The aim is to condense the whole project report into a few sentences without omitting any essential information. This means that there must be an introduction to the subject; aim of the research; identification of the research problem; questions or hypotheses; possibly setting and subjects; research methodology; research methods employed; results of analysis and conclusions arrived at; and perhaps the significance of the work. How long should an abstract be? For refereed journal, technical or conference papers the publishers/organizers usually stipulate a maximum of 150–250 words. For an undergraduate or master's dissertation it can be a little bit longer, but not usually more than about 300–400 words, and for a MPhil or PhD thesis, this will be extended to about a maximum one page of text. Always consult your publication or project brief to check on the requirements.

Here are some annotated examples from different disciplines and from different publications that give you a guide to the construction and content of actual abstracts. Notice that each sentence has a function. You can of course also consult and compare those that you find in your literature research on your own topic.

A journal paper abstract

Defining Criteria for Intervention in Earthen Built Heritage Conservation
Mariana Rosado Correia and Nicholas Walliman (2014).

Abstract

This paper examines the criteria for the procedural process that is applied to prevent decay in earthen built heritage conservation, referred to as intervention (*Subject in a nutshell*). When defining criteria for intervention, it was necessary first to establish what 'needs' are required to be addressed and then to define a 'methodology of intervention' while considering 'indicators of quality' and 'indicators of best practice' (*Research problem*). The aim is to contribute to a successful conservation approach, in order to better address 'threats' (*Main aim of research*). The research methodology of this investigation was based in a case study strategy using qualitative methods (*Research methodology*). Data was collected using documentary, questionnaire and interview methods from three sources, the case studies, the stakeholders and a selected group of international key-experts in earthen built heritage conservation (*Research methods*). Seven key components were identified for the methodology of intervention and the criteria for intervention were examined through three types of approach: descriptive, evaluative and prescriptive (*Results of analysis*). It was found that there was a serious lack of understanding amongst experts in conservation of the meaning and need for a methodology of intervention in conservation and the meaning or need for devising criteria for conservation (*Conclusions*).

A very short technical paper abstract

Cooled Floor Slabs Using Water: Dynamic modelling on a whole building scale.

Christopher Kendrick (2014) (unpublished paper).

Abstract

This paper details the development of a method for modelling the performance of a water-cooled slab cooling system in a commercial building using dynamic thermal simulation software (IES Apache), and outlines values of internal comfort conditions and energy use (*Aim, problem and methods all in one sentence!*). The cooling power of the system for 9am to 6pm operation was calculated at 16.9 W/m^2 (*Results*). Methods used to develop control strategies for embedded pipe slab cooling systems are suggested (*Another outcome*). It is concluded that this cooling system can, with suitable controls, economically eliminate overheating in a typical naturally ventilated open-plan office building (*Conclusions*).

And here is one from a master's dissertation

The Impact of Lean Thinking on the Online Marketing of Startups. Viktor Weber (2015).

Abstract

The goal of this dissertation is to analyse the impact of lean thinking on the online marketing of startups and to present a basic framework for lean, entrepreneurial online marketing, which should benefit academia as well as practitioners (*Research aim*). By conducting an extensive literature review, covering lean thinking, entrepreneurial marketing and online marketing theory, a profound knowledge level and concise synthesis can be presented, which informs the primary research (*Background research*). In order to create the aforementioned framework a grounded theory approach is pursued, by collecting primary data in an ethnographic study with semi-structured, one-to-one, in-depth interviews with a purposive sample of eleven entrepreneurs or Chief Marketing Executives (*Research methodology and data collection methods*). The sample consists of six startups from the United Kingdom and five from Germany (*sampling*).

After having transcribed the interviews, the data output is coded with NVivo 10, which leads to the new lean, entrepreneurial online marketing framework (*Data analysis methods*). Core findings are the emergence of four vital pillars in lean, entrepreneurial online marketing, which are online marketing with social media marketing and blogging, marketing analytics, networking and word of mouth marketing. It becomes evident that Facebook, Twitter and LinkedIn are the preferred social media, but require diligent monitoring and content production, which is also valid for blogging (*Results of the analysis*). Suitable key performance indicators, metrics and constant monitoring are essential to enhance marketing and develop the company's solution using customer feedback. Word of mouth should be incentivized intelligently via social media or referral programmes. Interestingly, networking cannot be solely conducted online but with events (*Conclusions and recommendations*).

Even though this paper could build an academic bridge between academia and practice, it could be improved by interviewing more entrepreneurs from various countries, which could be considered as limitation as well as chance for future research (*Limitation of the study*). Concluding, it can be stated that this framework has to be adequately adapted to each business environment of a company (*Instructions for further research*).

MAINTAINING YOUR MOTIVATION

There is no doubting that doing an individual research project for the first time is a demanding task that will, as it is meant to, stretch your personal resources while providing you with many opportunities to learn new skills and gain extra knowledge and understanding of both yourself and your subject. There will be times when your energy slumps, you question the wisdom of your decisions and you are daunted by all the work that still needs to be done. Here are some useful guidelines of how to avoid a crisis and how to cope if one does occur.

The main source of motivation is your interest in the topic being investigated. As it is your choice of topic, make sure that it is sufficiently fascinating to keep your attention for the duration of the study. It is often possible to link your research to one of your hobbies or activities outside academia, e.g. the physics of waves and surfboarding, the psychology of fashion, the implications for society of social networking. Additional motivation is gained by the relevance of what you are researching to aspirations regarding the future direction of your career. Careful choice of topic is therefore a fundamental issue.

With regard to your work habits, it is good to know whether you are a morning or night person – a lark or an owl, or something in-between. There is evidence that there is no justification for believing that Benjamin Franklin's maxim 'early to bed and early to rise makes a man healthy, wealthy, and wise' is sound (Gale and Martyn, 1998). Knowing when you can concentrate most and work more easily will help you to integrate your research efforts into your daily routine effectively. Don't wait for inspiration – it has often been noted that professional authors invariably work regular hours at their word processors, at whatever time of the day or night that might be. Inspiration comes with writing. Anyway, you will not be engaged in creative writing, your task will be more to generate a convincing evidence-based argument that supports your conclusions. This requires a methodical approach that can be easily planned, even if it is rather more difficult to achieve.

Keep some time for leisure, especially some exercise which takes you away from your desk or sofa. It is well known that exercise refreshes the spirit and promotes better energy levels. The static nature of working at a computer over long periods is bad for your health, so avoid leaving your work to the last minute – I know, easier said than done! At least take short breaks. A good way to do this is to make limited target for your work session, whether it is writing a section, analysing a set of data or compiling a diagram, etc. that needs only 2–3 hours to complete. When completed, this will provide you with a sense of achievement and a deserved rest.

The last chapter is always the biggest challenge. You will be tired from all the work you have done so far, probably rather fed up with concentrating so long on one subject, and keen to submit, especially if the deadline is looming. But it is this last chapter that is the climax of your work and your individual contribution to knowledge. It requires a lot of thought and imagination to draw all the evidence together to construct a sound argument in order to support a clear set of conclusions, carefully related to the initial aims of the study. This takes time, so to avoid stress at this stage you need to have allowed a big enough slot in your programme, and to have kept up with your plan of work.

If, at any time you 'hit the buffers' and don't know how to proceed, or just think you might be going the wrong way, don't wait – consult with your supervisor. There is no shame in encountering difficulties. Your supervisor will certainly have experienced similar situations, so should be able to give you useful advice on how to proceed. A view from outside your problem can often reveal a simple way out – there may be several alternative routes to progress.

QUALITY OF WORK

The dissertation or thesis is usually the culminating output after years of study, and you will want it to be a publication that represents the best of your work and something to be proud of. There are several measures you can take to help in this ambition.

Before you start your writing, it is advisable to look at previous successful dissertations or theses of your level of study in your subject area so that you can gauge the standard of work you need to achieve. Look at the structure of the work, the formulation of the research aims, questions or hypotheses, the sequence and contents of the chapters, the consistency of the argument, the way that evidence is compiled to make a case, and the technical aspects of the writing – use of headings, illustrations, paragraph structure, citation and referencing, use of appendices, lists of contents and figures, etc. You can then use the best and most relevant ones as models for your work. But don't be afraid to adjust the format to suite your own subject material – you will know best how to communicate effectively.

In order to make it easier to produce an attractive and consistent written work, do make the effort to learn how to use all the facilities of your word processing program, such as spellchecker, thesaurus, cut, paste, search, replace, page and text formatting, footnoting, page numbering, headings, captioning, generation of tables of contents and figures, citing and referencing, etc. Use the 'online help' facility if you get stuck, and don't hesitate to ask your more experienced colleagues for advice. The same goes for any other program you use for producing maps, illustrations, spreadsheets, diagrams and figures. Again, allocate time in your programme if you know that you will need training and practice.

If you are not writing in your first language, you face the added difficulty of producing text that is idiomatic, with correct grammar and spelling. Unfortunately, online translation programs are not yet sophisticated enough to produce translations of sufficiently high quality and accuracy for academic work. The best way to ensure that your writing reads well and is correctly structured is to get an intelligent native speaker (ideally a writer too) to review and correct your written work. You may be able to persuade a colleague to do this, but for best results you might have to pay for a professional proofreader. Many universities and colleges recognize the difficulties faced by overseas students from different language countries and provide specific help and advice on writing.

Your supervisor will be able to give you feedback on the quality of your work, but only if you show what you have done, in writing. He/she will be able to comment on the use of language, the consistency of the argument, the suitability of your research methods, and the clarity of presentation of the results of your investigations, and much more. Don't think that having to revise your work is a sign of failure. Redrafting is a normal activity. Writing and developing ideas always takes time, and there are several reasons for redrafting, for example, to adjust the length, clarify arguments, improve grammar and spelling, eliminate repetitions and re-order the sequence of headings.

Doing high-quality research takes time, so the biggest danger for achieving good results is leaving things till the last minute and having to rush to produce your submission. To avoid this, do follow the advice on careful planning, time management, reviewing and revision processes. Having enough time to do the best you can will result in an accurate assessment of your abilities.

WHERE TO FIND OUT MORE

There are plenty of books with advice for students for different aspects of study. Here is a selection of books that will provide more information on different aspects of writing:

Greetham, B. (2013) *How to Write Better Essays* (Palgrave Study Skills) (third edition). Basingstoke: Palgrave.
This practical guide addresses each landmark stage of the essay writing process with sections on analysing the question, brainstorming, evaluation and criticism, writing styles, and planning and structuring, as well as avoiding plagiarism.

Redman, P. (2013) *Good Essay Writing: A Social Sciences Guide* (fourth edition). London: Sage, in association with the Open University.
This shows you how to approach different types of essay questions, provides detailed guidelines on the various ways of supporting and sustaining key arguments, addresses common worries, and provides extensive use of worked examples, including complete essays which are fully analysed and discussed.

Shields, M. (2010) *Essay Writing: A Student's Guide*. London: Sage.
This offers practical, in-depth guidance on each of the stages of essay writing, reading academic texts, how to get the most out of lectures, referencing and citations, fluency and appropriateness of style and language.

And for information more aligned to writing up a dissertation or research project, try these books:

Thody, A. (2006) *Writing and Presenting Research*. London: Sage.
A practical, example-driven approach that shows you how to write up, report and publish research findings, not just as dissertations, but also as papers, books, articles and teaching presentations.

Wolcott, H. (2009) *Writing Up Qualitative Research* (third edition). London: Sage.
Good, down to earth, and easy to understand for both undergraduates and graduates.

Monippally, P. and Shankar, B. (2010) *Academic Writing: Guide for Management Students and Researchers*. Delhi: Sage.

Three main aspects are focused on: understanding existing research, documenting and sharing the results of the acquired knowledge, and acknowledging the use of other people's ideas and works in the documentation.

If you are an overseas student writing in your secondary language:

Bailey, S. (2014) *Academic Writing: A Handbook for International Students* (fourth edition). Abingdon: Routledge.

If you want to maximize your academic potential you will find this practical and easy-to-use book an invaluable guide to writing in English for your degree course.

Bailey, S. (2014) *Academic Writing for International Students of Business* (second edition). Abingdon: Routledge.

If you are an overseas student studying a business or economics course in English you might prefer this one. This book is especially designed to assist you by explaining the writing process from start to finish and helping you to practise all the key writing skills.

GLOSSARY

Abstractness   A characteristic of research findings that makes them independent from specific time and place. Such research findings are useful as they can be applied to other situations.

Accidental sampling   Also called convenience sampling. A non-random sampling technique that involves selecting what is immediately available, e.g. studying the building you happen to be in, examining the work practices of your firm.

Algorithm   A process or set of rules used for calculation or problem solving, especially using a computer. These can be expressed graphically or, more often, as a mathematical formula. An example is a formula that summarizes the interior conditions that lead to the feeling of climatic comfort, with factors such as air temperature, humidity, air movement, amount of clothing, etc.

Analogy   A comparison of two different types of thing to detect the similarities between them. It may be possible to infer that they possess further undetected similarities.

Argument   A type of discourse that not only makes assertions but also asserts that some of these assertions are reasons for others. Argument is often based on the rules of logic, in order to provide a solid structure.

Assertive discourse   A type of discourse that contains assertive statements, e.g. this man is bald.

Associational statements   Make an assertion that two concepts are associated in some way, positively, negatively, or not associated at all. The word 'correlation' is often employed to refer to the degree of association.

Authentication   Checking on historical data to verify whether it is authentic. Typical techniques used are textual analysis, carbon dating, paper analysis, cross-referencing, etc.

Axiomatic theory   A theory that comprises an initial set of statements (axioms) or self-evident truths, each independent of the others, and from which it is possible to logically derive all the other statements (propositions) of the theory. A good example of one of these is Pythagorean geometry.

Bell curve   Also known as a 'normal' or Gaussian curve. A common parameter of populations, where there is a preponderance of values to group around the centre, with progressively fewer towards the extremes. The basic characteristic required by parametric statistical analysis.

Bias   A distortion of a statistical or other analytical result due to a factor not allowed for in the calculations. This can be due to human or other influences. Often referred to in sampling methods.

Bibliographic database   An electronic list of bibliographic information. These may be on CD-ROM, or online on the Internet. Many of these are available through university and other libraries and can be searched using keywords, subjects, authors, titles, etc.

Bibliography   A list of key information about publications. These can be compiled on particular subjects or in relation to a particular piece of academic work. There are standard systems for compiling bibliographies, e.g. Harvard. Libraries usually compile their own bibliographies to guide students to literature in their particular subject.

Bivariate analysis   The analysis of two variables as to whether and to what extent they influence each other.

Categorization   Involves forming a typology of object, events or concepts. This can be useful in explaining what 'things' belong together and how.

Causal process theory   An interrelated set of definitions and statements which not only define the theory, but describe when and where the causal processes are expected to occur, and explain the causal processes or mechanisms by identifying the effect of the independent variables on the dependent variables.

Causal statements   These make an assertion that one concept or variable causes another – a 'cause and effect' relationship.

This can be deterministic, meaning that under certain conditions an event will inevitably follow, or, if the outcome is not so certain, probabilistic, meaning that an event has a certain chance (which may be quantifiable) of following.

Central tendency   A descriptive statistic that gives the measurement of location of, most commonly, the mean, median and mode of a data set. These are different types of 'average'.

Citation   A reference to a source of information or quotation given in a text. This is usually in abbreviated form to enable the full details to be found in the list of references.

Class   A set of persons or things grouped together or graded or differentiated from others. Classes can be formed by collection or division. Classes can be divided into sub-classes to form a hierarchy.

Cluster sampling   The selection of cases in a population that share one or several characteristics, but are otherwise as heterogeneous as possible, e.g. travellers using a railway station. Also known as area sampling when random segments are chosen from a large area of population distribution.

Coding   The application of labels or tags to allocate units of meaning to collected data. This is an important aspect of forming typologies and facilitates the organization of copious data in the form of notes, observations, transcripts, documents, etc. It helps to prevent 'data overload' resulting from mountains of unprocessed data in the form of ambiguous words. Coding of qualitative data can form a part in theory building. Codes can also be allocated to responses to fixed-choice questionnaires.

Coefficient of correlation   The measure of a statistical correlation between two or more variables. There are many types of these, the 'Pearsonian r' being the most common.

Concept   A general expression of a particular phenomenon, or words that represent an object or an idea. This can be concrete, e.g. dog, cat, house; or abstract – independent of time or place, e.g. anger, marginality, politics. We use concepts to communicate our experience of the world around us.

Conceptual scheme theory   Conceptual schemes that designate, or even prescribe, what constitute the characteristics of 'social facts'.

Consistency   A quality of argument concerned with the compatibility of beliefs, i.e. a set of beliefs that can be shown to be consistent with each other is said to be consistent.

Control   Having the ability to determine the influences on variables in a phenomenon, for example in an experiment. The crucial issue in control is to understand how certain variables affect one another, and then to be able to change the variables in such a way as to produce predictable results. Not all phenomena can be controlled, as many are too complex or not sufficiently understood.

Critical rationalism   An approach usually associated with Popper (1992) that maintains that rival theories can be judged against specific, unchanging, universal criteria, which are divorced from or set beyond the influences of time or society.

Critical realism   A non-empirical (i.e. realist) epistemology that maintains the importance of identifying the structures of social systems, even if they are not amenable to the senses. This will enable the structures to be changed to ameliorate social ills.

Data   The plural of datum, a specific measured value of a variable.

Data reduction   Techniques used to summarize the most significant or interesting features of a mass of qualitative data, the results of which are often shown in the form of matrices or networks.

Deduction   The inferring of particular instances from a general law, i.e. 'theory then research' approach.

Dependent variable   A variable that is expected to be affected by a manipulation of the independent variable.

Descriptive statistics   A method of quantifying the characteristics of parametric numerical data, e.g. where the centre is, how broadly they are spread, the point of central tendency, the mode, median and means. These are often explained in relation to a Gaussian (bell) curve.

Dichotomous   A nominal measure of data with only two categories, e.g. male/female, up/down.

Directive language   Language used for the purposes of causing or preventing overt action.

Discourse   Communication in the form of words as speech or writing or even attitude and gesture.

Discourse analysis   Studies the way people communicate with each other through language in a social setting, where language is not seen as a neutral medium for transmission of information, but is loaded with meanings displaying different versions of reality.

Empirical generalization   A generalization based on several empirical studies that reveal a similar pattern of events. All concepts in an empirical generalization must be directly measurable.

Empirical relevance   The measure of the correspondence between a particular theory and what is taken to be objective empirical data.

Epistemology   The theory of knowledge, especially about its validation and the methods used. Often used in connection with one's epistemological standpoint – how one sees and makes sense of the world.

Ethics   The rules of conduct. In this book, particularly about conduct with other people and organizations, aimed at causing no harm and providing, if possible, benefits.

Evaluation   Making judgements about the quality of objects or events. Quality can be measured either in an absolute sense or on a comparative basis.

Existence statements   These claim that instances of a concept exist in the real world, and provide a typology or a description.

Experience   Actual observation or practical acquaintance with facts or events that results in knowledge and understanding.

Explanation   One of the common objectives of research.

Expressive language   Language used to express emotions and feelings.

External reality   Acceptance of the reliability of knowledge gained by experience to provide empirical evidence.

External validity   The extent of the legitimate generalizability of the results of an experiment.

Falsification   The process by which a hypothesis is rejected as a result of true observational statements which conflict with it.

Focus group   A group of people assembled to discuss a particular subject of the research in order to reveal their opinions and beliefs. Usually they are selected for their relevant expertise or involvement in the subject.

Formal fallacies   These occur due to some error in the structure of the logic used, causing the chain of reasoning to be defective.

Frequency distribution   The values of the variables and their percentages of the total of variable values, usually displayed from the lowest to the highest values in a table.

Generality   The assumption that there can be valid relationships between the particular cases investigated by the researcher and other similar cases in the world at large.

Grounded theory   A type of research that develops theory on the basis of reciprocal phases of qualitative data collection, analysis and theory building, each phase informing the next.

Hypothesis   A theoretical statement that has not yet been tested against data collected in a concrete situation, but which it is possible to test by providing clear evidence for support or rejection.

Hypothetico–deductive method   Synonymous with scientific method. Progress in scientific thought by the four-step method of: identification of a problem, formulation of a hypothesis, practical or theoretical testing of the hypothesis, rejection or adjustment of hypothesis if it is falsified.

Idealism   An epistemological stance that maintains that the world exists, but that different people construe it in different ways. Each has his/her own reality.

Independent variable   A variable that, when it is manipulated, causes an effect or change on a dependent variable.

Index journal   Catalogues of the bibliographic details of journal articles without further details apart from, perhaps, keywords.

Indicator   A measure or sign, not usually directly measurable, that characterizes a concept.

Induction   The inference of a general law from particular instances. Our experiences lead us to make conclusions from which we generalize.

Inferential statistics   Statistical analysis that goes beyond describing the characteristics of the data and the examination of correlations of variables to produce predictions through inference based on the data analysed. Inferential statistics are also used to test statistically based hypotheses.

Informal fallacies   These occur when: the ambiguities of language admit error to an argument; something is left out that is needed to sustain an argument; irrelevant factors are permitted to weigh on the conclusions; or unwarranted presumptions alter the conclusion.

Informative language   Language used to communicate information.

Informed consent   Consent given by participants to take part in a research project based on having sufficient information about the purposes and nature of the research and the involvement required.

Interim summary A short report prepared about one-third of the way through data collection in qualitative research in order to review the quantity and quality of the data, confidence in its reliability, and the presence and nature of any gaps or puzzles that have been revealed, and to judge what still needs to be collected in the time available.

Internal validity A measure of the level of sophistication of the design and extent of control in an experiment. The values of data gained should genuinely reflect the influences of the controlled variables.

Interpretation An integral part of the analysis of data that requires verification and extrapolation to make out or bring out the meaning.

Interpretivism The standpoint that recognizes the 'embedded' nature of the researcher, and the unique personal theoretical stances upon which each person bases his/her actions. It rejects the assertion that human behaviour can be codified in laws by identifying underlying regularities, and that society can be studied from a detached, objective and impartial viewpoint by the researcher. Attempts to find understanding in research are mediated by our own historical and cultural milieu.

Intersubjectivity Agreement between people about meaning of concepts used in statements, attained by precise definition of the concepts. Intersubjectivity is also promoted by the use of appropriate logical systems such as mathematics, statistics and symbolic logic.

Interval level (of quantification) The use of equal units of measurement, but without a significant zero value, e.g. the Fahrenheit or Centigrade temperature scales.

Journal of abstracts Catalogues of the bibliographic details of journal articles together with summaries of articles (indicative or informative abstracts). These are often devoted to specific subject areas.

Laws Statements that describe relationships that are so well supported by evidence, and confidence in their reliability is so strong, that they are considered to express the 'truth' in the cases to which they apply.

Levels of abstraction   The degree of abstraction of a statement based on three levels – theoretical, operational and concrete, the last being the least abstract.

Levels of measurement   The four different types of quantification, especially when applied to operational definitions, namely nominal, ordinal, interval and ratio.

Library catalogue   Bibliographic details of items in a library. The databases are now usually accessed by computer as online public access catalogues (OPACs).

Logical truth   (when referring to statements) Logically true statements can be divided into three varieties: trivial (obvious), true by necessity (according to rules, e.g. mathematical) and true by definition (conforming to unambiguous definition).

Materialism   An epistemological stance that insists that only physical things and their interactions exist and that our minds and consciousness are wholly due to the active operation of materials.

Matrices   Two-dimensional arrangements of rows and columns used to summarize substantial amounts of information. They can be used to record variables such as time, levels of measurement, roles, clusters, outcomes, effects, etc. Latest developments allow the formulation of three-dimensional matrices.

Memos   Short analytical descriptions based on the developing ideas of the researcher reacting to the data and the development of codes and pattern codes. Compiling memos is a good way to explore links between data and to record and develop intuitions and ideas.

Meta-analysis   An overall analysis gained by drawing together the results of individual analysed components of the research, typically qualitative research.

Model   (a) A term used to describe the overall framework that we use to look at reality, based on a philosophical stance (e.g. postmodernism, post-structuralism, positivism, empiricism, etc.); (b) a simplified physical or mathematical representation of an object or a system used as a tool for analysis. It may be able to be manipulated to obtain data about the effects of the manipulations.

Networks   Maps or charts used to display data, made up of blocks (nodes) connected by links. They can be produced in a wide variety of formats, each with the capability of displaying different types of data, e.g. flow charts, organization charts, causal networks, mind maps, etc.

Nominal level (of quantification) The division of data into separate categories by naming or labelling.

Null hypothesis A statistically based hypothesis tested by using inferential statistics. A null hypothesis suggests no relationship between two variables.

Operational definition A set of actions that an observer should perform to detect or measure a theoretical concept. Operational definitions should be abstract, i.e. independent of time and space.

Order The condition that things are constituted in an organized fashion that can be revealed through observation.

Ordinal level (of quantification) Ordering data by rank without reference to specific measurement, i.e. more or less than, bigger or smaller than.

Paradigm The overall effect of the acceptance of a specific general theoretical approach, and the influence it has on the scientists' view of the world. According to Kuhn (1970), normal scientific activity is carried out within the terms of the paradigm.

Parameter A measurable characteristic or feature that is shared in different populations.

Parsimony Economy of explanation of phenomena, especially in formulating theories.

Participant Someone who takes part in a research project as a subject of study. This term implies that the person takes an active role in the research by performing actions or providing information.

Pilot study A pre-test of a questionnaire or other type of survey on a small number of cases in order to test the procedures and quality of responses.

Plagiarism The taking and use of other people's thoughts or writing as your own. This is sometimes done by students who copy out chunks of text from publications or the Internet and include it in their writing without any acknowledgement of its source.

Population A collective term used to describe the total quantity of cases of the type which are the subject of the study. It can consist of objects, people and even events.

Positivism An epistemological stance that maintains that all phenomena, including social, can be analysed using scientific method. Everything can be measured and, if only one knew enough, the causes and effects of all phenomena could be uncovered.

Postmodernism A movement that reacts against the all-embracing theories of the modern movement and insists on the inseparable links between knowledge and power.

Prediction One of the common objectives of research.

Primary data Sources from which researchers can gain data by direct, detached observation or measurement of phenomena in the real world, undisturbed by any intermediary interpreter. It is a matter of philosophical debate as to what extent the detachment and undisturbed state are possible or even desirable.

Problem area An issue within a general body of knowledge or subject from which a research project might be selected.

Proportional stratified sampling Used when cases in a population fall into distinctly different categories (strata) of a known proportion of that population.

Proposition A theoretical statement that indicates the clear direction and scope of a research project.

Quantification (of concepts) Measurement techniques used in association with operational definitions.

Quota sampling An attempt to balance the sample by selecting responses from equal numbers of different respondents. This is an unregulated form of sampling, as there is no knowledge of whether the respondents are typical of their class.

Ratio level (of quantification) A scale with equal units of measurement and containing a true zero equal to nought – the total absence of the quantity being measured.

Reasoning A method of coming to conclusions through the use of logical argument.

Regression A type of statistical analysis that uses simple and multiple predictions to predict Y from X values. Usually shown as a line through the values plotted on a scattergram.

Relational statements These impart information about a relationship between two concepts. They form the bedrock of scientific knowledge and explain, predict and provide us with a sense of understanding of our surroundings.

Relativism   The stance that implies that judgement is principally dependent on the values of the individuals or society and the perspectives from which they make their judgement. No universal criteria can be 'rationally' applied, and an understanding of decisions made by individuals or organizations can only be gained through knowledge of the historical, psychological and social backgrounds of the individuals.

Reliability   In relation to human perception and intellect, the power of memory and reasoning to organize data and ideas to promote understanding.

Research problem   A general statement of an issue meriting research. It is usually used to help formulate a research project and is the basis on which specific research questions, hypotheses or statements are based.

Research question   A theoretical question that indicates a clear direction and scope for a research project.

Sample   The small part of a whole (population) selected to show what the whole is like. There are two main types of sampling procedure, random and non-random.

Sampling error   The differences between the random sample and the population from which it has been selected.

Scientific method   The foundation of modern scientific enquiry. It is based on observation and testing of the soundness of conclusions commonly by using the hypothetico-deductive method. The four-step method is: identification of a problem; formulation of a hypothesis; practical or theoretical testing of the hypothesis; rejection or adjustment of hypothesis if it is falsified.

Secondary sources   Sources of information that have been subject to interpretation by others, usually in the form of publications.

Semiotics   The study of signs. A type of analysis, particularly of text and visual material, intent on revealing hidden or implicit meanings.

Sense of understanding   A complete explanation of a phenomenon provided by a wider study of the processes that surround, influence and cause it to happen.

Set of laws theory   A theory that comprises a set of separate, though interrelated, laws.

Significance (statistical)   The quality of the difference between the value of a case compared with that of a population, and how much the difference varies from values expected to have occurred by chance. A big difference from the chance values indicates increased statistical significance.

Simple random sampling   A method used to select cases at random from a uniform population.

Simple stratified sampling   A method that recognizes the different strata in the population in order to select a representative sample.

Simulation   The re-creation of system or process in a controllable form, usually using computers, to manipulate the variables in order to study their effects.

Snowball technique   Building up a sample by beginning with a core of known people or elements and increasing it by adding new people or elements given by members of the original sample. This is analogous to increasing the size of a snowball by rolling it down a snow-covered slope.

Statement   An assertion based on a combination of concepts.

Subject   The participant in a research project. The term implies a passive role in the project, i.e. that things are done to the subject in the form of a test or an experiment.

Sub-problem   A component of a main problem, usually expressed in less abstract terms to indicate an avenue of investigation.

Symbol   A sign used to communicate concepts in the form of natural or artificial language.

Systematic sampling   A sampling method that selects samples using a numerical method, e.g. the selection of every tenth name on a list.

Term   A word used to express a definite concept. It can be primitive, which cannot be described by using other terms, or derived, which can.

Theoretical sampling   Selection of a sample of the population that you think knows most about the subject. This approach is common in qualitative research where statistical inference is not required.

Theory   A system of ideas based on interrelated concepts, definitions and propositions, with the purpose of explaining or predicting phenomena.

Typology   An ordering of cases or data according to types and specific characteristics.

Validity   The property of an argument to correctly draw conclusions from premises according to the rules of logic.

Value   An actual measurement of a variable.

Variable   A measurable attribute of an indicator or a case.

Variance   The values of the variables compared with the mean. The greater the dispersion of values, the greater the variance of the data set.

Venn diagram   A diagram of overlapping circles used to analyse arguments.

BIBLIOGRAPHY

Barry, A., Born, G. and Weszkalnys, G. (2008) 'Logics of Interdisciplinarity'. *Economy and Society*, 37(1): 20–49.

Biggam, J. (2008) *Succeeding with Your Master's Dissertation: A Step-by-Step Handbook*. Basingstoke: Palgrave.

Blumer, H. (1969) *Symbolic Interactionism: Perspective and Method*. Englewood Cliffs, NJ: Prentice-Hall.

Bonnett, A. (2001) *How to Argue*. Harlow: Pearson Education.

Brink-Budgen, R. (2009) *Critical Thinking for Students: Learn the Skills of Critical Assessment and Effective Argument* (fourth edition). Oxford: How To Books.

Bromley, D.B. (1986) *The Case-Study Method in Psychology and Related Disciplines*. Chichester: Wiley.

Bryman, A. (2008) *Social Research Methods* (third edition). Oxford: Oxford University Press.

Bryman, A. and Cramer, D. (2008) *Quantitative Data Analysis with SPSS Release 14, 15 and 16: A Guide for Social Scientists*. London: Routledge.

Burdess, N. (2010) *Starting Statistics: A Short, Clear Guide*. London: Sage.

Byrne, D. (2002) *Interpreting Quantitative Data*. London: Sage.

Chalmers, A. (1999) *What Is This Thing Called Science?* (third edition). Milton Keynes: Open University Press.

Clark, V.L.P. and Creswell, J.W. (2008) *The Mixed Methods Reader*. Thousand Oaks, CA: Sage.

Clavin, A. (2010) *The Wellbeing Impacts of Ecologically Designed Community Gardens: A Capability Approach*. PhD thesis, Oxford Brookes University.

Coffey, A. and Atkinson, P. (1996) *Making Sense of Qualitative Data: Complementary Research Strategies*. London: Sage.

Collier, A. (1994) *Critical Realism: An Introduction to Roy Bhaskar's Philosophy*. London: Verso.

Cooper, D.R. and Schindler, P.S. (2009) *Business Research Methods* (tenth edition). New York: McGraw-Hill.

Crano, W., Brewer, M. and Lac, A. (2014) *Principles and Methods of Social Research* (third edition). New York: Routledge.

Cunningham, S. (n.d.) 'Archive Skills and Tools for Historians'. Making History article. Retrieved 2 February 2017 from: www.history.ac.uk/makinghistory/resources/articles/archive_skills_and_tools_for_historians.html.

David, M. and Sutton, C. (2004) *Social Research: The Basics*. London: Sage.

Densin, N. (2010) 'Moments, Mixed Methods, and Paradigm Dialogs'. *Qualitative Inquiry*, 16(6): 419–27.

Diamond, I. and Jeffries, J. (2000) *Beginning Statistics: An Introduction for Social Scientists*. London: Sage.

Dochartaigh, N. (2007) *Internet Research Skills: How to Do Your Literature Search and Find Research Information Online* (second edition). London: Sage.

Feyerabend, P. (1993) *Against Method: Outline of an Anarchistic Theory of Knowledge* (third edition). London: Verso.

Finke, A. (2010) *Conducting Research Literature Reviews: From the Internet to Paper* (third edition). London: Sage.

Fisher, A. (1998) *The Logic of Real Arguments*. Cambridge: Cambridge University Press.

Flick, U. (2009) *An Introduction to Qualitative Research* (fourth edition). London: Sage.

Forster, N. (1994) 'The Analysis of Company Documentation', in C. Cassell and G. Symon (eds), *Qualitative Methods of Organizational Research: A Practical Guide*. London: Sage, pp. 147–66.

Foucault, M. (1972) *The Archaeology of Knowledge*. London: Tavistock.

Gale, C. and Martyn, C. (1998) 'Larks and Owls and Health, Wealth, and Wisdom'. *BMJ*, 317(7174): 1675–7.

Gensler, H.J. (1989) *Logic: Analyzing and Appraising Arguments*. London: Prentice-Hall International.

Gibbons, J. (1992) *Nonparametric Statistics: An Introduction* (Quantitative Applications in the Social Sciences). Newbury Park, CA: Sage.

Glaser, B. and Strauss, A. (1967) *The Discovery of Grounded Theory: Strategies for Qualitative Research*. New York: Aldine de Gruyter.

Greene, J., Caracelli, V. and Graham, W. (1989) 'Toward a Conceptual Framework for Mixed-Method Evaluation Designs'. *Educational Evaluation and Policy Analysis*, 11(3): 255–74.

Greetham, B. (2008) *How to Write Better Essays* (Palgrave Study Skills). Basingstoke: Palgrave.

Hart, C. (2001) *Doing a Literature Search: A Comprehensive Guide for the Social Sciences*. London: Sage.

Heaton, J. (2004) *Reworking Qualitative Data: The Possibility of Secondary Analysis*. London: Sage.

Hodges, W. (2001) *Logic: An Introduction to Elementary Logic* (second edition). London: Penguin.

Holliday, A. (2007) *Doing and Writing Qualitative Research* (second edition). London: Sage.

Hoy, W. (2009) *Quantitative Research in Education: A Primer.* London: Sage.

Hughes, J. and Sharrock, W. (1997) *The Philosophy of Social Research* (third edition). Harlow: Longman.

Johnson, R., Onwuegbuzie, A. and Turner, L.A. (2007). 'Toward a Definition of Mixed Methods Research'. *Journal of Mixed Methods Research*, 1(2): 112–33.

Kerr, A., Hall, H. and Kozub, S. (2002) *Doing Statistics with SPSS.* London: Sage.

Kiecolt, J. and Nathan, L. (1986) *Secondary Analysis of Survey Data* (Sage University Papers). Newbury Park, CA: Sage.

Kozak, D. (2008) *Urban Fragmentation in Buenos Aires: The Case of Abasto.* PhD thesis, Oxford Brookes University.

Kuhn, T.S. (1970) *The Structure of Scientific Revolutions* (second edition). Chicago: Chicago University Press.

Laine, M. de. (2000) *Fieldwork, Participation and Practice: Ethics and Dilemmas in Qualitative Research.* London: Sage.

Leedy, P.D. and Ormrod, J. (2009) *Practical Research: Planning and Design* (ninth edition). Harlow: Pearson.

Lee-Treweek, G. and Linkogle, S. (eds) (2000) *Danger in the Field: Ethics and Risk in Social Research.* London: Routledge.

Locke, L.F. (2007) *Proposals that Work: A Guide for Planning Dissertations and Grant Proposals* (fifth edition). London: Sage.

Lorence, J. (1981) *The Critical Analysis of Documentary Evidence: Basic Skills in the History Classroom.* Paper presented at the American Historical Association – Ninety-Sixth Annual Meeting, December 28–30, 1981 Los Angeles. Retrieved 2nd February 2017 from: http://files.eric.ed.gov/fulltext/ED214813.pdf.

Machi, L. (2009) *The Literature Review: Six Steps to Success.* London: Corwin/Sage.

Mauthner, M. (ed.) (2002) *Ethics in Qualitative Research.* London: Sage.

Mertens, D.M. (1998) *Research Methods in Education and Psychology: Integrating Diversity with Quantitative & Qualitative Approaches.* Thousand Oaks, CA: Sage.

Miles, M.B. and Huberman, A.M. (1994) *Qualitative Data Analysis: An Expanded Sourcebook.* London: Sage.

Monippally, P. and Shankar, B. (2010) *Academic Writing: Guide for Management Students and Researchers.* Delhi: Sage.

Nissani, M. (1997) 'Ten Cheers for Interdisciplinarity: The Case for Interdisciplinary Knowledge and Research'. *Social Science Journal*, 34(2): 201–16.

Okasha, S. (2002) *Philosophy of Science: A Very Short Introduction.* Oxford: Oxford University Press.

Oliver, P. (2003) *The Student's Guide to Research Ethics.* Maidenhead: Open University Press.

O'Neill, T. (2015) *What is the Most Common 'Historical Method' Used by Historians Today?* Retrieved 23 February 2017 from: www.quora.com/What-is-the-most-common-historical-method-used-by-historians-today.

Onwuegbuzie, A. (2012) 'Putting the MIXED Back into Quantitative and Qualitative Research in Educational Research and Beyond: Moving Toward the Radical Middle'. *International Journal of Multiple Research Approaches*, 6(3): 192–219.

Pirie, M. (2007) *How to Win Every Argument: The Use and Abuse of Logic*. London: Continuum.

Popper, K. (1992) *The Logic of Scientific Discovery*. Routledge Classics. London: Routledge.

Punch, K. (2006) *Developing Effective Research Proposals*. London: Sage.

Redman, P. (2005) *Good Essay Writing: A Social Sciences Guide* (third edition). London: Sage, in association with the Open University.

Richie, J. and Lewis, J. (2003) *Qualitative Research Practice: A Guide for Social Science Students and Researchers*. London: Sage.

Ridley, D. (2008) *The Literature Review: A Step-by-Step Guide for Students*. London: Sage.

Robson, C. (2010) *Real World Research: A Resource for Social Scientists and Practitioner-Researchers* (third edition). Oxford: Blackwell.

Rosado Correia, M. and Walliman, N.R. (2014) 'Defining Criteria for Intervention in Earthen-Built Heritage Conservation'. *International Journal of Architectural Heritage*, 8(4): 581–601.

Rudestam, K.E. and Newton, R. (2007) *Surviving Your Dissertation: A Comprehensive Guide to Content and Process* (third edition). Thousand Oaks, CA: Sage.

Sale, J., Lohfeld, L. and Brazil, K. (2002) 'Revisiting the Quantitative–Qualitative Debate: Implications for Mixed-Methods Research'. *Quality and Quantity*, 36(1): 43–53.

Salkind, N. (2009) *Statistics for People Who (Think They) Hate Statistics* (second edition). Thousand Oaks, CA: Sage.

Salmon, M.H. (2007) *Introduction to Logic and Critical Thinking* (fifth edition). Belmont, CA: Wadsworth.

Samangooei, M. (2017) *Design Strategies for Food Production Integrated within Buildings in the UK*. PhD thesis, Oxford Brookes University.

Schwandt, T. (2007) *Qualitative Enquiry: A Dictionary of Terms* (third edition). Thousand Oaks, CA: Sage.

Seale, C. (ed.) (2004) *Researching Society and Culture* (second edition). London: Sage.

Seale, C., Gobo, G., Gubrium, J. and Silverman, D. (2004) *Qualitative Research Practice*. London: Sage.

Shields, M. (2010) *Essay Writing: A Student's Guide*. London: Sage.

Silverman, D. (1993) *Interpreting Qualitative Data: Methods for Analysing Talk, Text and Interaction*. London: Sage.

Smith, J. (1983) 'Quantitative versus Qualitative Research: An Attempt to Clarify the Issue'. *Educational Researcher*, 12(3): 6–13.

Symonds, J. and Gorard, S. (2008) *The Death of Mixed Methods: Research Labels and their Casualties*. Paper presented at the British Educational Research Association Annual Conference, Heriot Watt University, Edinburgh, 3–6 September.

Stewart, D. and Kamins, M. (1993) *Secondary Research Information Sources and Methods* (second edition). Thousand Oaks, CA: Sage.

Swetnam, D. (2000) *Writing Your Dissertation: How to Plan, Prepare and Present Successful Work* (third edition). Oxford: How To Books.

Tait, J. and Lyall, C. (2007) Short Guide to Developing Interdisciplinary Research Proposals. *ISSTI Briefing Note*, 1.

Tashakkori, A. and Teddlie, C. (2003) 'Issues and Dilemmas in Teaching Research Methods Courses in Social and Behavioural Sciences: US Perspective'. *International Journal of Social Research Methodology*, 6(1): 61–77.

Thody, A. (2006) *Writing and Presenting Research*. London: Sage.

Thompson, M. (2006) *Philosophy* (Teach Yourself). London: Hodder.

Thouless, R.H. (1974) *Straight and Crooked Thinking* (revised edition). London: Pan Books.

Vithal, R. and Jansen, J. (2012) *Designing Your First Research Proposal: A Manual for Researchers in Education and the Social Sciences* (second edition). Cape Town: Juta.

Walker, A. (2017) *Professionalism and Leadership: A Study of International Humanitarian and Development Organisations in South Asia*. Forthcoming PhD thesis, Oxford Brookes University.

Walliman, N. (2004) *Your Undergraduate Dissertation: The Essential Guide for Success*. London: Sage.

Walliman, N. (2005) *Your Research Project: A Step-by-Step Guide for the First-Time Researcher* (second edition). London: Sage.

Warburton, N. (2004) *Philosophy: The Basics* (fourth edition). London: Routledge.

Weber, V. (2015) *The Impact of Lean Thinking on the Online Marketing of Startups*. MSc thesis, Oxford Brookes University.

Wolcott, H. (2009) *Writing Up Qualitative Research* (third edition). London: Sage.

Wright, D.B. (2009) *First (and Second) Steps in Statistics*. London: Sage.

Yanchar, S. and Williams, D. (2006). 'Reconsidering the Compatibility Thesis and Eclecticism: Five Proposed Guidelines for Method Use'. *Educational Researcher*, 35(9): 3–12.

INDEX